Civil Rights Litigation: Cases and Perspectives

Third Edition

2007 Supplement

Roy L. Brooks
Warren Distinguished Professor of Law
University of San Diego

Gilbert Paul Carrasco
Professor of Law
Willamette University College of Law

Michael Selmi
Professor of Law
George Washington University Law School

Carolina Academic Press
Durham, North Carolina

ISBN: 978-1-59460-473-7

Carolina Academic Press
700 Kent Street
Durham, North Carolina 27701
Telephone (919) 489-7486
Fax (919) 493-5668
E-mail: cap@cap-press.com
www.cap-press.com

Casebook Page | Supplement Page

TABLE OF CONTENTS

CHAPTER 1
INTRODUCTION TO THE AMERICAN RACE PROBLEM

CHAPTER 2
THE RIGHT TO EQUAL EDUCATIONAL OPPORTUNITY

CHAPTER 3
PUBLIC ACCOMMODATIONS AND HOUSING

CHAPTER 4
EMPLOYMENT DISCRIMINATION

CHAPTER 5
THE RIGHT TO VOTE

CHAPTER 6
ADMINISTRATION OF JUSTICE

CHAPTER 7
CONSTITUTIONAL TORTS

CHAPTER 8
THE RIGHTS OF LANGUAGE MINORITIES

CHAPTER 9
THE RIGHTS OF PEOPLE WITH DISABILITIES

CHAPTER 10
AFFIRMATIVE ACTION

Table of Cases

Table of Secondary Authorities

Harassment By Supervisors As The Casual Nexus For The Discriminatory Motivating Factor In Mixed Motive Cases, 1993 Wisc. L. Rev. 231 (1993), 46

Jordan, Emma Coleman & Angela Harris, Economic Justice: Race, Gender, Identity and Economics (2005), 30

Karlan, Pamela S., Convictions and Doubts: Retribution, Representation and the Debate Over Felon Disenfranchisement, 56 Stan. L. Rev. 1147 (2004), 50

Lempert, Richard O. , Affirmative Action in American Law Schools: A Critical Response to Richar Sander's "A Reply to Critics," University of Michigan, John M. Olin Center for Law & Economics Working Paper 60 (February 24, 2006), 79

Levine, David I., Public School Assignment Methods After *Grutter* and *Gratz*: The View from San Francisco, 30 Hastings Const. L. Q. 511 (2003), 19

Manza, Jeff & Christopher Uggen, Locked Out: Felon Disenfranchisement and American Democracy (2006), 51

Merida, Kevin and Michael A. Fletcher, *Supreme Discomfort: The Divided Soul of Clarence Thomas* 67 (2007), 1

Miccio, G. Kristin, A House Divided: Mandatory Arrest, Domestic Violence, and the Conservatization of the Battered Women's Movement, 42 Hous. L. Rev. 237 (2005), 71

Miles, Thomas J., Felon Disenfranchisement and Voter Turnout, 33 Journal L. Studies 85 (2004), 51

Overton, Spencer, Voter Identification, 105 Mich. L. Rev. 631 (2007), 50

Parker, Wendy, Lessons in Losing: Race Discrimination in Employment, 81 Notre Dame L. Rev. 889 (2006), 30

Sander, Richard, A Reply to Critiques, 57 Stan. L. Rev. 1963 (2005), 79

Sander, Richard H., A Systemic Analysis of Affirmative Action in American Law Schools, 57 Stan. L. Rev. 367 (2004), 79

Secunda, Paul M., At the Crossroads of Title IX and a New "IDEA": Why Bullying Need Not Be "A Normal Part of Growing Up" For Special Education Children, 12 Duke J. Gender L. & Pol'y 1 (2005), 22

Selmi, Michael, Was the Disparate Impact Theory a Mistake?, 53 UCLA L. Rev. 701 (2006), 48

Shelby, Tommie, We Who Are Dark: The Philosophical Foundations of Black Solidarity (2005), 1

Smiley, Tavis ,ed., The Covenant with Black America (2006), 1

Strahilevitz, Loir Jacob, Exclusionary Amenities in Residential Communities, 92 Va. L. Rev. 437 (2006), 24

Thomas, Kenneth L. & Ramadanah M. Salaam, The Face of Title IX: Post Jackson v. Birmingham Board of Education, 66 Ala. Law. 429 (2005), 5

Selmi, Michael, Was the Disparate Impact Theory a Mistake?, 53 UCLA L. Rev. 701 (2006)

Waterstone, Michael, Constitutional and Statutory Voting Rights for People with Disabilities,14 Stan. L. & Pol. Rev. 353 (2003), 76

Yuracko, Kimberly A., Trait Discrimination as Race Discrimination: An Argument About Assimilation, 74 Geo. Wash. L. Rev. 365 (2006), 32

Winegar, Melanie, Note: Big Talk, Broken Promises: How Title I of the Americans with Disabilities Act Failed Disabled Workers, 34 Hofstra L. Rev. 1267 (2006), 76

CHAPTER 1

INTRODUCTION TO THE AMERICAN RACE PROBLEM

Add the following paragraph just before Section 1 Classical Liberalism, on page 13:

What is the best way to assess competing civil rights perspectives? In *We Who Are Dark: The Philosophical Foundations of Black Solidarity* (2005), Tommie Shelby argues that civil rights theory "must not be utopian—applicable only in an ideal world—but must be politically viable given the sociohistorical circumstances of contemporary black Americans." Id. at 250. On the other hand, it could be argued that civil rights theory must be have conceptual clarity and moral direction. Political instincts often cloud our moral judgments or our ability to reason linearly. Abolitionism was more coherent even though far less politically feasible than the separate-and-unequal civil rights policy during slavery. Formal equal opportunity was more coherent even though less politically feasible than the separate-but-equal civil rights theory during Jim Crow. In each case, society had to grow into a morally superior civil rights theory. See Roy L. Brooks, *Civil Rights Theory* (forthcoming 2007).

Add the following sentence at the end of the first full paragraph on page 16:

For a useful compendium of structural barriers African American face, see *The Covenant with Black America*, Tavis Smiley, ed. (New York: Third World Press, 2006).

Add the following at the end of the last paragraph on page 26:

Is Justice Thomas a limited separatist at heart? Thomas attended St. Pius X High School, an all-black Catholic high school in Savannah, Georgia. The school closed in 1971, having become a casualty of integration. After becoming a Supreme Court justice, Thomas reflected on the closure of St. Pius and hundreds of other black schools that took place in the 1970s. Justice Thomas remarked, "It broke my heart to see St. Pius close. Some people think that the solution to all the problems of black people is integration. I never worshipped at the alter [of integration]." Kevin Merida and Michael A. Fletcher, *Supreme Discomfort: The Divided Soul of Clarence Thomas* 67 (2007).

CHAPTER 2

THE RIGHT TO EQUAL EDUCATIONAL OPPORTUNITY

Add the following at the end of Note 6 on page 100:

For a summary of the distribution of burdens, see *Holton v. City of Thomasville School District*, 425 F.3d 1325 (11th Cir. 2005).

Add the following at the end of the Note on Equal Educational Opportunity in Contexts Not Involving Racial Segregation, on page 101:

Racine Charter One, Inc. v. Racine Unified School Dist. involved a Wisconsin school district that refused to bus students attending an independent charter school in the district. 424 F.3d 677 (7th Cir. 2005). The charter school alleged that the district was violating the Fourteenth Amendment by refusing to transport charter students solely because they were enrolled in the charter school. The Seventh Circuit held that equal protection was not implicated because the charter students were not similarly situated to the district's other students receiving transportation. The court focused on the difference between the charter school and the district's other public and private schools. The charter school was established by the University of Wisconsin through a unique state statute, and was operated independently from the other public schools in the district. State and local law obligated the district to provide transportation for public and private school students *within the district*, and the court found that the charter school's autonomous nature made it the functional equivalent of an independent school district. Thus, charter students were not similarly situated to students attending the district's public and private schools for the purpose of state and local transportation service. The court went on to find that, even if the charter students were similarly situated, the district's financial interest provided a rational basis for denying them transportation.

Add the following before the Notes on the Incremental Release of Court Supervision of the Desegregation Process on page 111:

Parents Involved in Community Schools v. Seattle School District No. 1

551 U.S. ___ , 2007 WL 1836531 (2007)

CHIEF JUSTICE ROBERTS announced the judgment of the Court, and delivered the opinion of the Court with respect to Parts I, II, III–A, and III–C, and an opinion with respect to Parts III–B and IV, in which JUSTICES SCALIA, THOMAS, and ALITO join.

The school districts in these cases voluntarily adopted student assignment plans that rely upon race to determine which public schools certain children may attend. The Seattle school district classifies children as white or nonwhite; the Jefferson County school district as black or "other." . . . In each case, the school district relies upon an individual student's race in assigning that student to a particular school, so that the racial balance at the school falls within a predetermined range based on the racial composition of the school district as a whole. Parents of students denied assignment to particular schools under these plans solely because of their race brought suit, contending that allocating children to different public schools on the basis of race violated the Fourteenth Amendment guarantee of equal protection. The Courts of Appeals below upheld the plans. We granted certiorari, and now reverse.

I

Both cases present the same underlying legal question — whether a public school that had not operated legally segregated schools or has been found to be unitary may choose to classify students by race and rely upon that classification in making school assignments. . . .

A

Seattle School District No. 1 operates 10 regular public high schools. In 1998, it adopted the plan at issue in this case for assigning students to these schools. App. In No. 05-908, pp. 90a-92a [footnote omitted]. The plan allows incoming ninth graders to choose from among any of the district's high schools, ranking however many schools they wish in order of preference. . . . If too many students list the same school as their first choice, the district employs a series of "tiebreakers" to determine who will fill the open slots at the oversubscribed school. The first tiebreaker selects for admission students who have a sibling currently enrolled in the chosen school. The next tiebreaker depends upon the racial composition of the particular school and the race of the individual student. . . . If an oversubscribed school is not within 10 percentage points of the district's overall white/nonwhite racial balance, it is what the district calls "integration positive," and the district employs a tiebreaker that selects for assignment students whose race "will serve to bring the school into balance." Id., at 38a. See *Parents Involved VII*, 426 F.3d 1162, 1169-1170 (CA9 2005) (en banc) [footnote omitted]. . . .

Seattle has never operated segregated schools — legally separate schools for students of different races — nor has it ever been subject to court-ordered desegregation. It nonetheless employs the racial tiebreaker in an attempt to address the effects of racially identifiable housing patterns on school assignments.

* * *

Petitioner Parents Involved in Community Schools (Parents Involved) is a nonprofit corporation comprising the parents of children who have been or may be denied assignment to their chosen high school in the district because of their race.

* * *

B

Jefferson County Public Schools operates the public school system in metropolitan Louisville, Kentucky. In 1973 a federal court found that Jefferson County had maintained a segregated school system . . . and entered a desegregation decree. Jefferson County operated under this decree until 2000, when the District Court dissolved the decree after finding that the district had achieved unitary status by eliminating "[t]o the greatest extent practicable" the vestiges of its prior policy of segregation. *Hampton v. Jefferson Cty. Bd. Of Ed.*, 102 F. Supp. 2d 358, 360 (2000). . . . In 2001, after the decree had been dissolved, Jefferson County adopted the voluntary student assignment plan at issue in this case. . . . The plan requires all nonmagnet schools to maintain a minimum black enrollment of 15 percent, and a maximum black enrollment of 50 percent. . . .

At the elementary school level, based on his or her address, each student is designated a "resides" school to which students within a specific geographic area are assigned; elementary resides schools are "grouped into clusters in order to facilitate integration." App. In No. 05-915, at 82. The district assigns students to nonmagnet schools in one of two ways: Parents of kindergartners, first-graders, and students new to the district may submit an application indicating a first and second choice among the schools within their cluster; students who do not submit such an application are assigned within the cluster by the district. "Decisions to assign students to schools within each cluster are based on available space within the schools and the racial guidelines in the District's current student assignment plan." Id., at 38. . . . If a school has reached the "extremes of the racial guidelines," a student whose race would contribute to the school's racial imbalance will not be assigned there. Id., at 38-39, 82. After assignment, students at all grade levels are permitted to apply to transfer between nonmagnet schools in the district. Transfers may be requested for any number of reasons, and may be denied because of lack of available space or on the basis of the racial guidelines.

* * *

II

[CHIEF JUSTICE ROBERTS for a Majority of the Court first rejected the Seattle school district's argument that the plaintiffs lacked standing.]

III

A

It is well established that when the government distributes burdens or benefits on the basis of individual racial classifications, that action is reviewed under strict scrutiny. *Johnson v. California*, 543 U. S. 499, 505–506 (2005); *Grutter v. Bollinger*, 539 U. S. 306, 326 (2003); *Adarand* [*Constructors v. Peña*, 515 U.S. 200, 224 (1995)]. . . . In order to satisfy this searching standard of review, the school districts must demonstrate that the use of individual racial classifications in the assignment plans hereunder review is "narrowly tailored" to achieve a "compelling" government interest. *Adarand*, supra, at 227. . . .

[O]ur prior cases, in evaluating the use of racial classifications in the school context, have recognized two interests that qualify as compelling. The first is the compelling interest of remedying the effects of past intentional discrimination. See *Freeman v. Pitts*, 503 U. S. 467, 494 (1992). Yet the Seattle public schools have not shown that they were ever segregated by law, and were not subject to court-ordered desegregation decrees. The Jefferson County public schools were previously segregated by law and were subject to a desegregation decree entered in 1975. In 2000, the District Court that entered that decree dissolved it, finding that Jefferson County had "eliminated the vestiges associated with the former policy of segregation and its pernicious effects," and thus had achieved "unitary" status. *Hampton*, 102 F. Supp. 2d, at 360. Jefferson County accordingly does not rely upon an interest in remedying the effects of past intentional discrimination in defending its present use of race in assigning students. . . . Once Jefferson County achieved unitary status, it had remedied the constitutional wrong that allowed race-based assignments. Any continued use of race must be justified on some other basis.

The second government interest we have recognized as compelling for purposes of strict scrutiny is the interest in diversity in higher education upheld in *Grutter*, 539 U. S., at 328. The specific interest found compelling in *Grutter* was student body diversity "in the context of higher education." Ibid. The diversity interest was not focused on race alone but encompassed "all factors that may contribute to student body diversity." Id., at 337.

* * *

The entire gist of the analysis in *Grutter* was that the admissions program at issue there focused on each applicant as an individual, and not simply as a member of a particular racial group. The classification of applicants by race upheld in *Grutter* was only as part of a "highly individualized, holistic review," 539 U.S., at 337. As the Court explained, "[t]he importance of this individualized consideration in the context of a race-conscious admissions program is paramount." Ibid. The point of the narrow tailoring analysis in which the *Grutter* Court engaged was to ensure that the use of racial classifications was indeed part of a broader assessment of diversity, and not simply an effort to achieve racial balance, which the Court explained would be "patently unconstitutional." Id., at 330.

In the present cases, by contrast, race is not considered as part of a broader effort to achieve "exposure to widely diverse people, cultures, ideas, and viewpoints," ibid.; race, for some students, is determinative standing alone. The districts argue that other factors, such as student preferences, affect assignment decisions under their plans, but under each plan when race comes into play, it is decisive by itself. It is not simply one factor weighed with others in reaching a decision, as in *Grutter*; it is *the* factor. . . .

Even when it comes to race, the plans here employ only a limited notion of diversity, viewing race exclusively in white/nonwhite terms in Seattle and black/"other" terms in Jefferson County. . . . [U]nder the Seattle plan, a school with 50 percent Asian-American students and 50 percent white students but no African-American, Native-American, or Latino students would qualify as balanced, while a school with 30 percent Asian-American, 25 percent African-American, 25 percent Latino, and 20 percent white students would not. . . .

Prior to *Grutter*, the courts of appeals rejected as unconstitutional attempts to implement race-based assignment plans — such as the plans at issue here — in primary and secondary schools. See, e.g., *Eisenberg v. Montgomery Cty. Public Schools*, 197 F. 3d 123, 133 (CA4 1999); *Tuttle v. Arlington Cty. School Bd.*, 195 F. 3d 698, 701 (CA4 1999); *Wessman v. Gittens*, 160 F. 3d 790, 809 (CA1 1998). See also *Ho v. San Francisco Unified School Dist.*, 147 F. 3d 854, 865 (CA9 1998). After *Grutter*, however, the two Courts of Appeals in these cases, and one other, found that race-based assignments were permissible at the elementary and secondary level, largely in reliance on that case. See *Parents Involved VII*, 426 F. 3d, at 1166; [*McFarland v. Jefferson Cty. Public Schools* (*McFarland II)*, 416 F. 3d 513], at 514 [(CA6 2005)]; *Comfort v. Lynn School Comm.*, 418 F. 3d 1, 13 (CA1 2005).

In upholding the admissions plan in *Grutter*, though, this Court relied upon considerations unique to institutions of higher education, noting that in light of "the expansive freedoms of speech and thought associated with the university environment, universities occupy a special niche in our constitutional tradition." 539 U. S., at 329. . . .The Court in *Grutter* expressly articulated key limitations on its holding — defining a specific type of broad-based diversity and noting the unique context of higher education — but these limitations were largely disregarded by the lower courts in extending *Grutter* to uphold race-based assignments in elementary and secondary schools. The present cases are not governed by *Grutter*.

B

[B]oth school districts assert additional interests, distinct from the interest upheld in *Grutter*, to justify their race-based assignments. . . . Seattle contends that its use of race helps to reduce racial concentration in schools and to ensure that racially concentrated housing patterns do not prevent nonwhite students from having access to the most desirable schools. . . . Jefferson County has articulated a similar goal, phrasing its interest in terms of educating its students "in a racially integrated environment." App. In No. 05-915, at 22 [footnote omitted]. Each school district argues that educational and broader socialization benefits flow from a racially diverse learning environment, and each contends that because the diversity they seek is racial diversity — not the broader diversity at issue in *Grutter* — it makes sense to promote that interest directly by relying on race alone. The parties and their amici dispute whether racial diversity in schools in fact has a marked impact on test scores and other objective yardsticks or achieves intangible socialization benefits. The debate is not one we need to resolve, however, because it is clear that the racial classifications employed by the districts are not narrowly tailored to the goal of achieving the educational and social benefits asserted to flow from racial diversity. In design and operation, the plans are directed only to racial balance, pure and simple, an objective this Court has repeatedly condemned as illegitimate.

The plans are tied to each district's specific racial demographics, rather than to any pedagogic concept of the level of diversity needed to obtain the asserted educational benefits. * * *

The districts offer no evidence that the level of racial diversity necessary to achieve the asserted educational benefits happens to coincide with the racial demographics of the respective school districts — or rather the white/nonwhite or black/"other" balance of the districts, since that is the only diversity addressed by the plans.

* * *

In *Grutter*, the number of minority students the school sought to admit was an undefined "meaningful number" necessary to achieve a genuinely diverse student body. 539 U. S., at 316, 335–336. [T]he majority concluded that the law school did not count back from its applicant pool to arrive at the "meaningful number" it regarded as necessary to diversify its student body. Id., at 335–336. Here the racial balance the districts seek is a defined range set solely by reference to the demographics of the respective school districts.

This working backward to achieve a particular type of racial balance, rather than working forward from some demonstration of the level of diversity that provides the purported benefits, is a fatal flaw under our existing precedent. We have many times over reaffirmed that "[r]acial balance is not to be achieved for its own sake." *Freeman*, 503 U.S., at 494. . . . *Grutter* itself reiterated that "outright racial balancing" is "patently unconstitutional." 539 U.S., at 330.

Accepting racial balancing as a compelling state interest would justify the imposition of racial proportionality throughout American society, contrary to our repeated recognition that "[a]t the heart of the Constitution's guarantee of equal protection lies the simple command that the Government must treat citizens as individuals, not as simply components of a racial, religious, sexual or national class." *Miller v. Johnson*, 515 U. S. 900, 911 (1995) (quoting *Metro Broadcasting* [*Inc. v. FCC*, 497 U. S. 547, at 602 (1990)] (O'Connor, J., dissenting); internal quotation marks omitted) [footnote omitted].

* * *

The Ninth Circuit below stated that it "share[d] in the hope" expressed in *Grutter* that in 25 years racial preferences would no longer be necessary to further the interest identified in that case. *Parents Involved VII*, 426 F. 3d, at 1192. But in Seattle the plans are defended as necessary to address the consequences of racially identifiable housing patterns. The sweep of the mandate claimed by the district is contrary to our rulings that remedying past societal discrimination does not justify race-conscious government action.

* * *

The principle that racial balancing is not permitted is one of substance, not semantics. Racial balancing is not transformed from "patently unconstitutional" to a compelling state interest simply by relabeling it "racial diversity." While the school districts use various verbal formulations to describe the interest they seek to promote — racial diversity, avoidance of racial isolation, racial integration — they offer no definition of the interest that suggests it differs from racial balance.

* * *

C

The districts assert, as they must, that the way in which they have employed individual racial classifications is necessary to achieve their stated ends. The minimal effect these classifications have on student assignments, however, suggests that other means would be effective. Seattle's racial tiebreaker results, in the end, only in shifting a small number of students between schools. In over one-third of the assignments affected by the racial tiebreaker, . . . the use of race in the end made no difference, and the district could identify only 52 students who were ultimately affected adversely by the racial tiebreaker in that it resulted in assignment to a school they had not listed as a preference and to which they would not otherwise have been assigned.

* * *

Similarly, Jefferson County's use of racial classifications has only a minimal effect on the assignment of students. . . . Jefferson County estimates that the racial guidelines account for only 3 percent of assignments. . . . While we do not suggest that greater use of race would be preferable, the minimal impact of the districts' racial classifications on school enrollment casts doubt on the necessity of using racial classifications.

* * *

The districts have also failed to show that they considered methods other than explicit racial classifications to achieve their stated goals. Narrow tailoring requires "serious, good faith consideration of workable race-neutral alternatives," *Grutter*, supra, at 339, and yet in Seattle several alternative assignment plans — many of which would not have used express racial classifications — were rejected with little or no consideration. . . . Jefferson County has failed to present any evidence that it considered alternatives, even though the district already claims that its goals are achieved primarily through means other than the racial classifications. . . .

IV

JUSTICE BREYER's dissent takes a different approach to these cases, one that fails to ground the result it would reach in law. . . . To begin with, JUSTICE BREYER seeks to justify the plans at issue under our precedents recognizing the compelling interest in remedying past intentional discrimination. . . . Not even the school districts go this far, and for good reason. The distinction between segregation by state action and racial imbalance caused by other factors has been central to our jurisprudence in this area for generations. . . .The dissent elides this distinction between de jure and de facto segregation, casually intimates that Seattle's school attendance patterns reflect illegal segregation, . . . and fails to credit the judicial determination — under the most rigorous standard — that Jefferson County had eliminated the vestiges of prior segregation.

* * *

JUSTICE BREYER's position comes down to a familiar claim: The end justifies the means. He admits that "there is a cost in applying 'a state-mandated racial label,'" . . . but he is confident that the cost is worth paying. Our established strict scrutiny test for racial classifications, however, insists on "detailed examination, both as to ends and as to means." *Adarand,* supra, at 236 (emphasis added). Simply because the school districts may seek a worthy goal does not mean they are free to discriminate on the basis of race to achieve it, or that their racial classifications should be subject to less exacting scrutiny.

* * *

In keeping with his view that strict scrutiny should not apply, JUSTICE BREYER repeatedly urges deference to local school boards on these issues. Such deference "is fundamentally at odds with our equal protection jurisprudence. We put the burden on state actors to demonstrate that their race-based policies are justified." *Johnson*, 543 U. S., at 506, n. 1. . . .

JUSTICE BREYER'S dissent ends on an unjustified note of alarm. It predicts that today's decision "threaten[s]" the validity of "hundreds of state and federal statutes and regulations.". . . But the examples the dissent mentions – for example, a provision of the No Child Left Behind Act that requires States to set measurable objectives to track the achievement of students from major racial and ethnic groups, 20 U.S.C. § 6311(b)(2)(C)(v) – have nothing to do with the pertinent issues in these cases.

JUSTICE BREYER also suggests that other means for achieving greater racial diversity in schools are necessarily unconstitutional if the racial classifications at issue in these cases cannot survive strict scrutiny. . . . These other means – e.g., where to construct new schools, how to allocate resources among schools, and which academic offerings to provide to attract students to certain schools – implicate different considerations than the explicit racial classifications at issue in these cases, and we express no opinion on their validity – not even in dicta.

* * *

Before *Brown* [*v. Board of Education*, 347 U.S. 483 (1954)], schoolchildren were told where they could and could not go to school based on the color of their skin. The school districts in these cases have not carried the heavy burden of demonstrating that we should allow this once again — even for very different reasons. For schools that never segregated on the basis of race, such as Seattle, or that have removed the vestiges of past segregation, such as Jefferson County, the way "to achieve a system of determining admission to the public schools on a nonracial basis," *Brown II*, 349 U. S. [294, at 300–301 (1955)], is to stop assigning students on a racial basis. The way to stop discrimination on the basis of race is to stop discriminating on the basis of race.

The judgments of the Courts of Appeals for the Sixth and Ninth Circuits are reversed, and the cases are remanded for further proceedings.

It is so ordered.

JUSTICE THOMAS, concurring.

Today, the Court holds that state entities may not experiment with race-based means to achieve ends they deem socially desirable. I wholly concur in THE CHIEF JUSTICE's opinion. I write separately to address several of the contentions in JUSTICE BREYER's dissent (hereinafter the dissent). Contrary to the dissent's arguments, resegregation is not occurring in Seattle or Louisville; these school boards have no present interest in remedying past segregation; and these race-based student-assignment programs do not serve any compelling state interest. Accordingly, the plans are unconstitutional. Disfavoring a color-blind interpretation of the Constitution, the dissent would give school boards a free hand to make decisions on the basis of race — an approach reminiscent of that advocated by the segregationists in *Brown v. Board of Education*, 347 U. S 483 (1954) This approach is just as wrong today as it was a half-century ago. * * *

JUSTICE KENNEDY, concurring in part and concurring in the judgment.

The Nation's schools strive to teach that our strength comes from people of different races, creeds, and cultures uniting in commitment to the freedom of all. In these cases two school districts in different parts of the country seek to teach that principle by having classrooms that reflect the racial makeup of the surrounding community. That the school districts consider these plans to be necessary should remind us our highest aspirations are yet unfulfilled. But the solutions mandated by these school districts must themselves be lawful. To make race matter now so that it might not matter later may entrench the very prejudices we seek to overcome. In my view the state-mandated racial classifications at issue, official labels proclaiming the race of all persons in a broad class of citizens—elementary school students in one case, high school students in another—are unconstitutional as the cases now come to us.

I agree with THE CHIEF JUSTICE that we have jurisdiction to decide the cases before us and join Parts I and II of the Court's opinion. I also join Parts III–A and III–C for reasons provided below. My views do not allow me to join the balance of the opinion by THE CHIEF JUSTICE, which seems to me to be inconsistent in both its approach and its implications with the history, meaning, and reach of the Equal Protection Clause. . . .

I

The plurality . . . does not acknowledge that the school districts have identified a compelling interest here. . . .For this reason, among others, I do not join Parts III–B and IV. Diversity, depending on its meaning and definition, is a compelling educational goal a school district may pursue.

It is well established that when a governmental policy is subjected to strict scrutiny, "the government has the burden of proving that racial classifications 'are narrowly tailored measures that further compelling governmental interests.'" *Johnson*, supra, at 505 (quoting *Adarand Constructors, Inc. v. Peña*, 515 U. S. 200, 227 (1995)). . . . The government bears the burden of justifying its use of individual racial classifications. As part of that burden it must establish, in detail, how decisions based on an individual student's race are made in a challenged governmental program. The Jefferson County Board of Education fails to meet this threshold mandate.

Petitioner Crystal Meredith challenges the district's decision to deny her son Joshua McDonald a requested transfer for his kindergarten enrollment. The district concedes it denied his request "under the guidelines," which is to say, on the basis of Joshua's race. Brief for Respondents in No. 05-915, p. 10; see also App. in No. 05-915, p. 97. Yet the district also maintains that the guidelines do not apply to "kindergartens," Brief for Respondents in No. 05-915, at 4, and it fails to explain the discrepancy.

* * *

The discrepancy identified is not some simple and straightforward error that touches only upon the peripheries of the district's use of individual racial classifications. To the contrary, Jefferson County in its briefing has explained how and when it employs these classifications only in terms so broad and imprecise that they cannot withstand strict scrutiny. . . . While it acknowledges that racial classifications are used to make certain assignment decisions, it fails to make clear, for example, who makes the decisions; what if any oversight is employed; the precise circumstances in which an assignment decision will or will not be made on the basis of race; or how it is determined which of two similarly situated children will be subjected to a given race-based decision.

* * *

Jefferson County fails to make clear to this Court — even in the limited respects implicated by Joshua's initial assignment and transfer denial — whether in fact it relies on racial classifications in a manner narrowly tailored to the interest in question, rather than in the far-reaching, inconsistent, and ad hoc manner that a less forgiving reading of the record would suggest. When a court subjects governmental action to strict scrutiny, it cannot construe ambiguities in favor of the State.

As for the Seattle case, the school district has gone further in describing the methods and criteria used to determine assignment decisions on the basis of individual racial classifications. . . . The district, nevertheless, has failed to make an adequate showing in at least one respect. It has failed to explain why, in a district composed of a diversity of races, with fewer than half of the students classified as "white," it has employed the crude racial categories of "white" and "non-white" as the basis for its assignment decisions.

* * *

Far from being narrowly tailored to its purposes, this system threatens to defeat its own ends, and the school district has provided no convincing explanation for its design. . . . As the district fails to account for the classification system it has chosen, despite what appears to be its ill fit, Seattle has not shown its plan to be narrowly tailored to achieve its own ends; and thus it fails to pass strict scrutiny.

II

Our Nation from the inception has sought to preserve and expand the promise of liberty and equality on which it was founded. Today we enjoy a society that is remarkable in its openness and opportunity. Yet our tradition is to go beyond present achievements, however significant, and to recognize and confront the flaws and injustices that remain. This is especially true when we seek assurance that opportunity is not denied on account of race. The enduring hope is that race should not matter; the reality is that too often it does. This is by way of preface to my respectful submission that parts of the opinion by THE CHIEF JUSTICE imply an all-too-unyielding insistence that race cannot be a factor in instances when, in my view, it may be taken into account. The plurality opinion is too dismissive of the legitimate interest government has in ensuring all people have equal opportunity regardless of their race. The plurality's postulate that "[t]he way to stop discrimination on the basis of race is to stop discriminating on the basis of race" . . . is not sufficient to decide these cases. Fifty years of experience since *Brown* v. *Board of Education*, 347 U. S. 483 (1954), should teach us that the problem before us defies so easy a solution. School districts can seek to reach *Brown*'s objective of equal educational opportunity. The plurality opinion is at least open to the interpretation that the Constitution requires school districts to ignore the problem of *de facto* resegregation in schooling. I cannot endorse that conclusion.

* * *

In the administration of public schools by the state and local authorities it is permissible to consider the racial makeup of schools and to adopt general policies to encourage a diverse student body, one aspect of which is its racial composition. Cf. *Grutter v. Bollinger*, 539 U. S. 306 (2003); id., at 387–388 (KENNEDY, J., dissenting). If school authorities are concerned that the student-body compositions of certain schools interfere with the objective of offering an equal educational opportunity to all of their students, they are free to devise race-conscious measures to address the problem in a general way and without treating each student in different fashion solely on the basis of a systematic, individual typing by race.

School boards may pursue the goal of bringing together students of diverse backgrounds and races through other means, including strategic site selection of new schools; drawing attendance zones with general recognition of the demographics of neighborhoods; allocating resources for special programs; recruiting students and faculty in a targeted fashion; and tracking enrollments, performance, and other statistics by race. These mechanisms are race conscious but do not lead to different treatment based on a classification that tells each student he or she is to be defined by race, so it is unlikely any of them would demand strict scrutiny to be found permissible.

* * *

In the cases before us it is noteworthy that the number of students whose assignment depends on express racial classifications is limited. I join Part III–C of the Court's opinion because I agree that in the context of these plans, the small number of assignments affected suggests that the schools could have achieved their stated ends through different means. These include the facially race-neutral means set forth above or, if necessary, a more nuanced, individual evaluation of school needs and student characteristics that might include race as a component. . . .

III

* * *

A

* * *

As the Court notes, we recognized the compelling nature of the interest in remedying past intentional discrimination in *Freeman v. Pitts*, 503 U.S. 467, 494 (1992), and of the interest in diversity in higher education in *Grutter*. At the same time, these compelling interests, in my view, do help inform the present inquiry. And to the extent the plurality opinion can be interpreted to foreclose consideration of these interests, I disagree with that reasoning.

* * *

B

To uphold these programs the Court is asked to brush aside two concepts of central importance for determining the validity of laws and decrees designed to alleviate the hurt and adverse consequences resulting from race discrimination. The first is the difference between *de jure* and *de facto* segregation; the second, the presumptive invalidity of a State's use of racial classifications to differentiate its treatment of individuals.

* * *

Yet, like so many other legal categories that can overlap in some instances, the constitutional distinction between *de jure* and *de facto* segregation has been thought to be an important one.

* * *

C

* * *

This Nation has a moral and ethical obligation to fulfill its historic commitment to creating an integrated society that ensures equal opportunity for all its children. A compelling interest exists in avoiding racial isolation, an interest that a school district, in its discretion and expertise, may choose to pursue. Likewise, a district may consider it a compelling interest to achieve a diverse student population. Race may be one component of that diversity, but other demographic factors, plus special talents and needs, should also be considered. . . .

The decision today should not prevent school districts from continuing the important work of bringing together students of different racial, ethnic, and economic backgrounds. . . .

JUSTICE STEVENS, dissenting.

While I join JUSTICE BREYER's eloquent and unanswerable dissent in its entirety, it is appropriate to add these words.

There is a cruel irony in THE CHIEF JUSTICE's reliance on our decision in *Brown v. Board of Education*, 349 U. S. 294 (1955). The first sentence in the concluding paragraph of his opinion states: "Before Brown, schoolchildren were told where they could and could not go to school based on the color of their skin." . . . THE CHIEF JUSTICE fails to note that it was only black schoolchildren who were so ordered; indeed, the history books do not tell stories of white children struggling to attend black schools. In this and other ways, THE CHIEF JUSTICE rewrites the history of one of this Court's most important decisions. * * *

It is my firm conviction that no Member of the Court that I joined in 1975 would have agreed with today's decision.

JUSTICE BREYER, with whom JUSTICE STEVENS, JUSTICE SOUTER, and JUSTICE GINSBURG join, dissenting.

These cases consider the longstanding efforts of two local school boards to integrate their public schools. The school board plans before us resemble many others adopted in the last 50 years by primary and secondary schools throughout the Nation. All of those plans represent local efforts to bring about the kind of racially integrated education that *Brown v. Board of Education*, 347 U. S. 483 (1954), long ago promised—efforts that this Court has repeatedly required, permitted, and encouraged local authorities to undertake. This Court has recognized that the public interests at stake in such cases are "compelling."

We have approved of "narrowly tailored" plans that are no less race-conscious than the plans before us. And we have understood that the Constitution *permits* local communities to adopt desegregation plans even where it does not *require* them to do so.

* * *

I

Facts

The historical and factual context in which these cases arise is critical. In *Brown*, this Court held that the government's segregation of schoolchildren by race violates the Constitution's promise of equal protection. . . . And it thereby set the Nation on a path toward public school integration.

In dozens of subsequent cases, this Court told school districts previously segregated by law what they must do at a minimum to comply with *Brown*'s constitutional holding. . . .Beyond those minimum requirements, the Court left much of the determination of how to achieve integration to the judgment of local communities.

* * *

Overall these efforts brought about considerable racial integration. More recently, however, progress has stalled. . . . As of 2002, almost 2.4 million students, or over 5% of all public school enrollment, attended schools with a white population of less than 1%. Of these, 2.3 million were black and Latino students, and only 72,000 were white. Today, more than one in six black children attend a school that is 99–100% minority. . . . In light of the evident risk of a return to school systems that are in fact (though not in law) resegregated, many school districts have felt a need to maintain or to extend their integration efforts.

* * *

In both Seattle and Louisville, the local school districts began with schools that were highly segregated in fact. In both cities plaintiffs filed lawsuits claiming unconstitutional segregation. In Louisville, a federal district court found that school segregation reflected pre-*Brown* state laws separating the races. In Seattle, the plaintiffs alleged that school segregation unconstitutionally reflected not only generalized societal discrimination and residential housing patterns, but also school board policies and actions that had helped to create, maintain, and aggravate racial segregation. In Louisville, a federal court entered a remedial decree. In Seattle, the parties settled after the school district pledged to undertake a desegregation plan. In both cities, the school boards adopted plans designed to achieve integration by bringing about more racially diverse schools. In each city the school board modified its plan several times in light of, for example, hostility to busing, the threat of resegregation, and the desirability of introducing greater student choice. And in each city, the school boards' plans have evolved over time in ways that progressively diminish the plans' use of explicit race-conscious criteria.

[JUSTICE BREYER provided a detailed history of the Seattle and Louisville school assignment plans.]

The histories I have set forth describe the extensive and ongoing efforts of two school districts to bring about greater racial integration of their public schools. In both cases the efforts were in part remedial. . . . The plans in both Louisville and Seattle grow out of these earlier remedial efforts. . . .When formulating the plans under review, both districts drew upon their considerable experience with earlier plans, having revised their policies periodically in light of that experience. . . .

The histories also make clear the futility of looking simply to whether earlier school segregation was *de jure* or *de facto* in order to draw firm lines separating the constitutionally permissible from the constitutionally forbidden use of "race-conscious" criteria. . . . [O]ur precedent has recognized that *de jure* discrimination can be present even in the absence of racially explicit laws. See *Yick Wo v. Hopkins*, 118 U. S. 356, 373– 374 (1886).

No one here disputes that Louisville's segregation was de jure. But what about Seattle's? Was it de facto? De jure? A mixture? Opinions differed. Or is it that a prior federal court had not adjudicated the matter? Does that make a difference? Is Seattle free on remand to say that its schools were de jure segregated, just as in 1956 a memo for the School Board admitted? The plurality does not seem confident as to the answer. . . .

A court finding of *de jure* segregation cannot be the crucial variable. After all, a number of school districts in the South that the Government or private plaintiffs challenged as segregated by law voluntarily desegregated their schools without a court order — just as Seattle did. . . .

* * *

II

The Legal Standard

A longstanding and unbroken line of legal authority tells us that the Equal Protection Clause permits local school boards to use race-conscious criteria to achieve positive race-related goals, even when the Constitution does not compel it. * * *

Courts are not alone in accepting as constitutionally valid the legal principle that [*North Carolina Bd. Of Ed. v.*] *Swann*, [402 U.S. 43 (1971)] enunciated – i.e., that the government may voluntarily adopt race-conscious measures to improve conditions of race even when it is not under a constitutional obligation to do so. That principle has been accepted by every branch of government and is rooted in the history of the Equal Protection Clause itself. Thus, Congress has enacted numerous race-conscious statutes that illustrate that principle or rely upon its validity. . . . In fact, without being exhaustive, I have counted 51 federal statutes that use racial classifications. I have counted well over

100 state statutes that similarly employ racial classifications. Presidential administrations for the past half-century have used and supported various race-conscious measures. . . .

There is reason to believe that those who drafted an Amendment with this basic purpose in mind would have understood the legal and practical difference between the use of race-conscious criteria in defiance of that purpose, namely to keep the races apart, and the use of race-conscious criteria to further that purpose, namely to bring the races together. See generally R. Sears, A Utopian Experiment in Kentucky: Integration and Social Equality at Berea, 1866-1904 (1996) (describing federal funding, through the Freedman's Bureau, of race-conscious school integration programs). See also R. Fischer, The Segregation Struggle in Louisiana 1862-77, p. 51 (1974) (describing the use of race-conscious remedies); Harlan, Desegregation in New Orleans Public Schools During Reconstruction, 67 Am. Hist. Rev. 663, 664 (1962) (same); W. Vaughn, Schools for All: The Blacks and Public Education in the South, 1865-1877, pp. 111-116 (1974) (same). Although the Constitution almost always forbids the former, it is significantly more lenient in respect to the latter. . . .

Sometimes Members of this Court have disagreed about the degree of leniency that the Clause affords to programs designed to include. See *Wygant v. Jackson Board of Education*, 476 U. S. 267, 274 (1986); *Fullilove v. Klutznick*, 448 U. S. 448, 507 (1980). But I can find no case in which this Court has followed JUSTICE THOMAS' "colorblind" approach. And I have found no case that otherwise repudiated this constitutional asymmetry between that which seeks to exclude and that which seeks to include members of minority races.

* * *

The upshot is that the cases to which the plurality refers, though all applying strict scrutiny, do not treat exclusive and inclusive uses the same. Rather, they apply the strict scrutiny test in a manner that is "fatal in fact" only to racial classifications that harmfully exclude; they apply the test in a manner that is not fatal in fact to racial classifications that seek to include.

* * *

The view that a more lenient standard than "strict scrutiny" should apply in the present context would not imply abandonment of judicial efforts carefully to determine the need for race-conscious criteria and the criteria's tailoring in light of the need. And the present context requires a court to examine carefully the race-conscious program at issue. . . .

In my view, this contextual approach to scrutiny is altogether fitting. . . . Nonetheless, in light of *Grutter* and other precedents, see, e.g., [*Regents of Univ. Of Cal. v.*] *Bakke*, 438 U. S. [265], at 290 [(1978)] (opinion of Powell, J.), I shall adopt the first alternative. I shall apply the version of strict scrutiny that those cases embody. I shall consequently ask whether the school boards in Seattle and Louisville adopted these plans to serve a "compelling governmental interest" and, if so, whether the plans are "narrowly tailored" to achieve that interest. If the plans survive this strict review, they would survive less exacting review a fortiori. Hence, I conclude that the plans before us pass both parts of the strict scrutiny test. Consequently I must conclude that the plans here are permitted under the Constitution.

III

Applying the Legal Standard

A

Compelling Interest

[JUSTICE BREYER described the interests he argued that the school assignment plans advanced].

In light of this Court's conclusions in *Grutter*, the "compelling" nature of these interests in the context of primary and secondary public education follows here *a fortiori*. Primary and secondary schools are where the education of this Nation's children begins, where each of us begins to absorb those values we carry with us to the end of our days. As Justice Marshall said, "unless our children begin to learn together, there is little hope that our people will ever learn to live together." *Milliken v. Bradley*, 418 U. S. 717, 783 (1974) (dissenting opinion).

* * *

The plurality tries to draw a distinction by reference to the well-established conceptual difference between *de jure* segregation ("segregation by state action") and *de facto* segregation ("racial imbalance caused by other factors"). . . .But that distinction concerns what the Constitution *requires* school boards to do, not what it *permits* them to do. . . . As to what is *permitted*, nothing in our equal protection law suggests that a State may right only those wrongs that it committed. . . .

Nor does any precedent indicate, as the plurality suggests with respect to Louisville . . . that remedial interests vanish the day after a federal court declares that a district is "unitary." . . . I do not understand why this Court's cases, which rest the significance of a "unitary" finding in part upon the wisdom and desirability of returning schools to local control, should deprive those local officials of legal permission to use means they once found necessary to combat persisting injustices.

* * *

B

Narrow Tailoring

I next ask whether the plans before us are "narrowly tailored" to achieve these "compelling" objectives. . . .Several factors, taken together . . . lead me to conclude that the boards' use of race-conscious criteria in these plans passes even the strictest "tailoring" test.

* * *

The school boards' widespread consultation, their experimentation with numerous other plans, indeed, the 40-year history that Part I sets forth, make clear that plans that are less explicitly race-based are unlikely to achieve the board's "compelling" objectives. The history of each school system reveals highly segregated schools, followed by remedial plans that involved forced busing, followed by efforts to attract or retain students through the use of plans that abandoned busing and replaced it with greater student choice. Both cities once tried to achieve more integrated schools by relying solely upon measures such as redrawn district boundaries, new school building construction, and unrestricted voluntary transfers. In neither city did these prior attempts prove sufficient to achieve the city's integration goals. . . .

Moreover, giving some degree of weight to a local school board's knowledge, expertise, and concerns in these particular matters is not inconsistent with rigorous judicial scrutiny. It simply recognizes that judges are not well suited to act as school administrators. Indeed, in the context of school desegregation, this Court has repeatedly stressed the importance of acknowledging that local school boards better understand their own communities and have a better knowledge of what in practice will best meet the educational needs of their pupils.

* * *

Finally, I recognize that the Court seeks to distinguish *Grutter* from these cases by claiming that *Grutter* arose in "'the context of higher education.'" . . .But that is not a meaningful legal distinction. I have explained why I do not believe the Constitution could possibly find "compelling" the provision of a racially diverse education for a 23-year-old law student but not for a 13-year-old high school pupil. . . .

The upshot is that these plans' specific features — (1)their limited and historically-diminishing use of race, (2) their strong reliance upon other non-race-conscious elements, (3) their history and the manner in which the districts developed and modified their approach, (4) the comparison with prior plans, and (5) the lack of reasonably evident alternatives — together show that the districts' plans are "narrowly tailored" to achieve their "compelling" goals. In sum, the districts' race-conscious plans satisfy "strict scrutiny" and are therefore lawful.

* * *

IV

Direct Precedent [omitted]

* * *

V

Consequences [omitted]

* * *

VI

Conclusions

* * *

Finally, what of the hope and promise of *Brown*? For much of this Nation's history, the races remained divided. It was not long ago that people of different races drank from separate fountains, rode on separate buses, and studied in separate schools. In this Court's finest hour, *Brown v. Board of Education* challenged this history and helped to change it. For *Brown* held out a promise. It was a promise embodied in three Amendments designed to make citizens of slaves. It was the promise of true racial equality — not as a matter of fine words on paper, but as a matter of everyday life in the Nation's cities and schools. It was about the nature of a democracy that must work for all Americans. It sought one law, one Nation, one people, not simply as a matter of legal principle but in terms of how we actually live.

* * *

To invalidate the plans under review is to threaten the promise of *Brown*. The plurality's position, I fear, would break that promise. This is a decision that the Court and the Nation will come to regret.

I must dissent.

APPENDIXES TO OPINION OF BREYER, J. [omitted]

Notes

1. The different opinions in *Parents Involved in Community Schools* each found support in *Brown v. Board of Education*. Chief Justice Roberts' plurality opinion and Justice Thomas' concurring opinion suggest that school assignment plans in which students' race dictates what school they attend represent the very practice that *Brown* sought to eliminate. Justice Kennedy's concurring opinion and both dissents, on the other hand, concluded that the plurality's approach prevents school districts from fulfilling *Brown*'s promise of ending unequal educational opportunities. Which argument is the most faithful to *Brown*?

2. Is the plurality opinion too dismissive of *Grutter v. Bollinger,* which upheld the University of Michigan Law School admissions program and found that achieving a diverse student body was a compelling state interest? *See* Chapter 10 at p. 1266 for an excerpt of *Grutter*. The plurality concluded that *Grutter* did not govern the Seattle and Louisville cases because *Grutter* was decided in the unique context of higher education and that, unlike the districts' assignment plans, the admissions program at the University of Michigan sought diversity in broader terms than based solely on race. Where docs this leave K-12 school districts? Can diversity in a broader sense serve as a compelling state interest at the K-12 level? Or does the plurality suggest that diversity as a compelling state interest is reserved only for higher education? If so, why is diversity more valuable at the higher education level than in K-12 schools? Is Justice Breyer correct in his dissent that the interests in school diversity at the university level follows "*a fortiori*" in the K-12 setting, where young people first begin to form their values?

3. Should the plurality opinion and Justice Kennedy's concurring opinion have applied a different, "more lenient" level of judicial review than traditional strict scrutiny, as Justice Breyer argued in his dissent? Should the scrutiny have been lessstrict because the school districts sought to include minority students rather than exclude them? Should K-12 school assignment plans in general receive a lesser level of review, given the difficult task that school districts face in having to assign, often with minimal resources, thousands of students to a school? *See* Deborah N. Archer, *Moving Beyond Strict Scrutiny: The Need for a More Nuanced Standard of Equal Protection Analysis for K Through 12 Integration Programs*, 9 U. PA. J. CONST. L. 629 (2007).

4. Chief Justice Roberts's plurality opinion distinguished the school district's method for assigning students from the "individualized, holistic" review approved of in *Grutter*. Is such a review even practical at the K-12 level? *See* David I. Levine, *Public School Assignment Methods After* Grutter *and* Gratz*: The View from San Francisco*, 30 HASTINGS CONST. L. Q. 511, 521 (2003) ("[I]t borders

on the absurd to imagine these hypothetical phalanxes of public school admissions officers purporting to conduct searching, individualized 'holistic reviews' of detailed files of millions of four-year-olds applying to kindergartens across the country"); see also Leslie Yalof Garfield, *Back to* Bakke: *Defining the Strict Scrutiny Test for Affirmative Action Policies Aimed at Achieving Diversity in the Classroom*, 83 Neb. L. Rev. 631 (2005) (arguing that a different strict scrutiny test should be used for evaluating affirmative action admissions policies than that used to evaluate affirmative action programs aimed at achieving diversity in the workplace).

5. Is Justice Thomas's concurring opinion consistent with his apparent support of limited separation as expressed in remarks regarding the closing of the all-black Catholic high school he attended in Savannah, Georgia, in the 1960s? See discussion of Justice Thomas as a limited separatist in Chapter 1.

Add the following at the end of Notes on the Incremental Release of Court Supervision of the Desegregation Process, on page 112:

Freeman identified a "causal link" between current racial imbalance and past *de jure* segregation. 503 U.S. at 496. In *Holton v. City of Thomasville School District*, 425 F.3d 1325 (2005), the Eleventh Circuit suggested that the causal link will be broken indefinitely when *de jure* segregation is cured, even if for a limited time. Thomasville County's schools were statutorily segregated until 1965, when the district began adopting its own plans for desegregation. District schools were desegregated for at least six consecutive years before a suit was brought. In deferring to the trial court's decision, the Eleventh Circuit held: "the district court, in this case, found that the District remedied the constitutional violation caused by its *de jure* segregated school system through the adoption of its 1970 desegregation plan, which, undeniably, successfully desegregated the District's school for a number of years. Subsequent demographic and enrollment changes, however, intervened, undoing much of the racial balance achieved by the 1970 desegregation plan. While the District is, of course, free to adopt attendance zones or other constitutional measures that might counteract these effects, it is simply beyond the authority of any court to force such a policy measure on the District." Id. at 1352.

Add the following new Note 5 after *Alexander v. Sandoval* on page 207:

5. Can a private school without federal funding racially discriminate when admitting applicants? The Supreme Court has held that it cannot. *Runyon v. McCrary*, 427 U.S. 160 (1976) (relying on the federal law that forbids racial discrimination in the making and enforcement of contracts, 42 U.S.C. § 1981). Nevertheless, the Ninth Circuit upheld the racially exclusive admission policy used by Hawaii's Kamehameha schools in the court's rehearing of *Doe v. Kamehameha Schools/Bernice Pauahi Bishop Estate*, 470 F.3d 8275 (9th Cir. 2006) (*en banc*), *cert. dismissed,* 127 S. Ct. 2160 (2007).

Established by a charitable trust from Hawaii's Princess Bernice Pauahi Bishop in 1887, the Kamehameha school system was intended to educate boys and girls of native Hawaiian ancestry. The school policy required that applicants for admission demonstrate academic qualifications, as well as proof of native ancestry. Applicants with at least some Hawaiian ancestry were admitted before even the most qualified of those who lacked native blood. A non-native brought suit against the school system and charitable trust, alleging the admission policy constituted unlawful racial discrimination in violation of § 1981. The school's interest in improving specific and significant imbalances in educational achievement of the target population, native Hawaiians, overcame the exclusively racial preference. The policy did not unnecessarily trammel the interests of others and it didno more than necessary to remedy the identified imbalances. The Civil Rights Act of 1866 (42 U.S.C. § 1981) is discussed in the context of public accommodations in the text at p. 268 *et seq.*, in the context of employment at p. 545 *et seq.*, and in the context of alienage and the rights of language minorities at p. 974 *et seq.*

Add the following at the end of the Note on page 217:

For more on *Jackson*, see Kenneth L. Thomas and Ramadanah M. Salaam, *The Face of Title IX: Post Jackson v. Birmingham Board of Education*, 66 Ala. Law. 429 (2005).

Add the following to Note 2 on page 259:

Davis provides some guidance by interpreting *Gebser* to require "deliberate indifference to *known acts* of harassment." 526 U.S. 629, 643 (emphasis added). Also interpreting *Gebser*, the Third Circuit held that actual notice required more than "information sufficient to alert" an appropriate official to the possibility that a teacher was involved in a sexual relationship with a student. *Bostic v. Smyrna School Dist.*, 418 F.3d 355 (2005). The Third Circuit's standard for actual notice was knowledge of facts "indicating sufficiently substantial danger to students." Id. at 361. Using this standard, the appellate court affirmed the trial court's finding that the court appropriately found administrators were not actually aware of a sexual relationship between a student and coach where the administrators' knowledge came from student rumors, one teacher's report that he saw the two standing closely together, and the parents' complaint that they found the two alone together in a car at night. Id.

An "appropriate official" is one who has actual notice of the misconduct and the authority to remedy it. For student-on-student harassment, teachers and counselors can be appropriate officials if they have the authority to stop the misconduct, perhaps by transferring a harassing student, suspending him, curtailing privileges, or providing additional supervision. *Jones v. Indiana Area School Dist.*, 397 F. Supp.2d 628, 643 (W.D.Pa. 2005) (interpreting *Gebser*, 524 U.S. at 291). For teacher-on-student harassment, can actual notice by a teacher or counselor be imputed to an administrator with the authority to stop the misconduct? See *Murrell v. School Dist. No. 1, Denver, Col.*, 186 F.3d 1238, 1247 (10th Cir. 1999).

When is an appropriate official "deliberately indifferent" to misconduct? In *Davis*, the Court held that a "clearly unreasonable" response to known misconduct was enough to constitute deliberate indifference. Id. at 649. A response is usually clearly unreasonable when it is unjustifiably delayed, or never even occurs. Does an official's failure to respond to past misconduct automatically give rise to deliberate indifference to future misconduct? See *Williams v. Board of Regents of University System of Georgia*, 477 F.3d 1282 (11th Cir.2007) (student-on-student harassment); *Zamora v. North Salem Cent. School Dist.*, 414 F.Supp.2d 418 (S.D.N.Y.2006) (teacher-on-student harassment).

Title IX states, in relevant part, that no person "shall *on the basis of sex*, be excluded from participation in, be denied the benefits of, or be subjected to discrimination under any education program or activity receiving Federal financial assistance." 20 U.S.C. § 1681(a) (emphasis added). Does this include same-sex harassment? At least two courts have found that same-sex harassment motivated by perceptions that a student was gay was actionable under Title IX. See *Theno v. Tonganoxie Unified School Dist. No.* 464, 394 F. Supp.2d 1299 (D.Kan. 2005); *Martin v. Swartz Creek Community Schools*, 419 F. Supp.2d 967 (E.D.Mich. 2006). In *Theno*, the court held that sexual gestures, innuendos, and name calling motivated by male students' belief that a fellow male student "failed to conform to stereotypical gender expectations for a teenage boy in their community," gave rise to gender discrimination. Id. at 1308. What if the gestures and comments were not motivated by perceptions that he was "effeminate or homosexual," but rather just teenage banter? Are the latter less dangerous? See Vanessa Eisemann, *Protecting the Kids in the Hall: Using Title IX to Stop Student-On-Student Anti-Gay Harassment*, 15 Berkeley Women's L.J. 125 (2000); Gilbert Paul Carrasco, *Sexuality and Discrimination: A Rights and Liberties Perspective* 255 (2005) (discussing sex stereotyping in the context of Title VII). Is Title IX the best framework for addressing bullying behavior targeted at special education children? See Paul M. Secunda, *At the Crossroads of Title IX and a New "IDEA": Why Bullying Need Not Be "A Normal Part of Growing Up" For Special Education Children,* 12 Duke J. Gender L. & Pol'y 1 (2005).

CHAPTER 3

PUBLIC ACCOMMODATIONS AND HOUSING

Add to the end of Note 2 on page 296:

See also Cleveland v. Capshaw Enterprises, ___ F. 3d ___, 74 U.S.L.W. 1732 (No. 05-4643-cv, 2d Cir. 2006). In *Capshaw Enterprises*, the plaintiffs, two African American college students, placed a deposit on an apartment and were ready to move in when they were informed that they would need to put down a larger deposit, that perhaps the plaintiffs were not "the right fit" for the apartment building because the "professional" living downstairs would not like having unruly college-age tenants living above him, and, finally, that the apartment had already been rented by another person. Slip op. at 3. The plaintiffs brought suit against the property management company, the company's representatives and the building's owner, Capshaw Enterprises. The court found that a building's owner could be vicariously liable for the actions of the property manager. The issue, according to the court, was to what extent the property manager was acting as an agent of the property owner.

Add as new Note 4 on page 297:

4. The internet has created a unique set of problems under the Fair Housing Act because it is often difficult to identify the cyberspace speaker. This problem is particularly evident when dealing with interactive housing websites, which receive direct federal protection under the Communications Decency Act (CDA). Congress' goal in adopting the CDA was to encourage the "unfettered and unregulated development of free speech on the internet." *Batzel v. Smith*, 333 F. 3d 1018, 1027 (9th Cir. 2003) (citing 47 U.S.C. § 230 (a)(3)-(4), (b)(1)-(2)). Thus, its purpose is seemingly in conflict with Title VIII.

Under the CDA, "[n]o provider . . . of an interactive computer service shall be treated as the publisher or speaker of any information provided by another information content provider." 47 U.S.C. § 230(C). Therefore, under this law, information service providers are immune from liability for content created by third parties. If a provider is responsible, however, in whole or in part for creating or developing the information, the provider is not entitled to the immunity. 47 U.S.C. § 230 (f)(3). The only way a plaintiff can state a claim under the CDA, therefore, is by showing that the internet service provider plays more than a passive role in disseminating the information.

The conflict between the CDA and Title VIII is implicated when internet service providers offer matching services whereby people find roommates over the internet. A violation of Title VIII may arise when such services are provided using discriminatory criteria to match potential roommates. In *Fair Housing Council of San Fernando Valley v. Roommates.com, LLC*, 2007 WL 1412650 (9th Cir. 2007), the court held that the defendant ("Roommate") was not immune under the CDA for the creation of allegedly discriminatory questionnaires it provided to its users. The website provided questionnaires that elicited preferences from categories of males, females, straight, gay, and/or lesbian. Failure to select from these categories resulted in inability to complete the registration process.

The Fair Housing Councils of San Fernando Valley and San Diego alleged that this was a "statement . . . with respect to the sale or rental of a dwelling that indicates . . . an intention to make [a] preference, limitation, or discrimination." *Roommates*, slip. op., at 3(citing 42 U.S.C. § 3604(C)). Remanding on the issue of whether there was a violation of Title VIII, the court rejected Roommate's argument that it was simply passing along information created by third parties. Instead, it held that, by categorizing, channeling, and limiting the distribution of users' profiles, Roommate provides an additional layer of information that it is responsible for, at least in part, creating or developing. *Roommates*, slip. op., at 5.

Add as new Note 5 on page 316:

5. Because the Fair Housing Act has made it increasingly difficult for developers and communities to discriminate against people of color, some developers have used new methods to discourage them from moving into neighborhoods. Amenities a developer may include in a development may have such exclusionary effects -- from golf courses to a community religious facility that all residents of the community have to help fund. On the other hand, some amenities can be viewed as inclusionary and may enhance heterogeneity in the community. Examples of these inclusionary amenities are a community pool or clubs that do not restrict membership in any way. Loir Jacob Strahilevitz, *Exclusionary Amenities in Residential Communities*, 92 Va. L. Rev. 437 (2006). Could such exclusionary amenities trigger a Title VIII challenge based on disparate impact analysis?

Add as new Note 3 on page 329:

3. In *Villas West II of Willowridge v. McGlothin*, 841 N.E.2d 584 (Ind. App. 2006) the Indiana court ruled that a homeowners association violated the Fair Housing Act by enforcing a restrictive covenant that prohibited a homeowner from leasing her property in the development. The community's rationale for the restriction was to maintain "the congenial and residential character of Villas West II and for the protection of owners with regard to financially responsible residents . . . ." The court found that the covenant worked a disparate impact on minorities and voided it.

Add as new Subsection C4. Discrimination in Insurance at page 337:

The phenomenon of red-lining has typically been conceived in relation to sale of housing or in financing, but it occurs in the context of homeowners insurance as well. Insurance, albeit a heavily regulated industry by states, is nevertheless subject to the requirements of the civil rights laws.

In Missouri, homeowner insurance companies must file their rates with the state regulatory agency. Such insurers are precluded from charging anything but the rate filed with the agency. As a result of this, potential insureds, it was argued, are prevented from claiming that the rates they are being charged, or will be charged, are unreasonable. The court in the following case dealt with the issue of whether the filing system in Missouri prevented a potential insured from having a claim of racial discrimination under the Fair Housing Act or under 42 U.S.C. §§ 1981 and 1982.

Saunders v. Farmers Insurance Exchange

440 F.3d 940 (8th Cir. 2006)

[942] Before LOKEN, Chief Judge, FAGG and BYE, Circuit Judges.

LOKEN, Chief Judge.

In 1996, numerous plaintiffs sued twenty-five insurers under the Fair Housing Act, 42 U.S.C. §§ 3601 et seq., and the Civil Rights Acts of 1866 and 1870, 42 U.S.C. §§ 1981 and 1982, seeking class action relief for defendants' allegedly discriminatory policies that deny homeowners insurance to the residents of minority neighborhoods in Missouri. The district court denied class certification and dismissed the complaint without prejudice, concluding that plaintiffs lack standing to bring claims against defendants against whom they have alleged no direct injury. We affirmed. *Canady v. Allstate Ins. Co.*, 1997 WL 33384270 (W.D. Mo. 1997), *aff'd*, 162 F.3d 1163 (8th Cir. 1998).

Plaintiffs then filed ten new actions, each asserting the same claims against a single *Canady* defendant. Warned by the district court that they "cannot establish a 'direct injury' without showing a 'direct contact' between the plaintiffs and the defendant," plaintiffs filed Revised Second Amended Complaints, each challenging a single defendant's alleged unlawful practices with respect to the marketing and underwriting of homeowners insurance in a single, contiguous black community in Kansas City. In *McClain v. American Econ. Ins. Co.*, 424 F.3d 728 (8th Cir. 2005) (McClain), we affirmed the dismissal of the complaints against three insurers for lack of standing. We now consider three separate appeals challenging the dismissal of complaints against three other insurers – Farmers Insurance Exchange (Farmers), American Family Mutual Insurance Company (American Family), and Shelter General Insurance Company (Shelter). These appeals raise an issue not raised in *McClain* – whether the district court properly applied the filed rate doctrine in dismissing claims that defendants' pricing policies and practices reflect unlawful race discrimination.

We reverse the dismissal of the pricing claims and otherwise affirm.

I. The Insurance Coverage Claims. [omitted]

***

II. The Price Discrimination Claims.

[943] Plaintiffs . . . allege that each defendant violated the Fair Housing Act and the Civil Rights Acts by "charg[ing] higher premium rates for the same type of homeowner's coverage to homeowners in the Community . . . than it has charged homeowners in white communities." The district court dismissed these price discrimination claims. Applying what has come to be known as the filed rate doctrine, the court held that, because homeowners insurers doing business in Missouri may only charge premium rates filed with the Missouri Department of Insurance, a ratepayer suffers no injury from being charged the filed rate. Therefore, the court reasoned, plaintiffs lack standing to claim that a different rate should have been charged. See *Keogh v. Chicago & N.W. Ry.*, 260 U.S. 156, 161-65 (1922). On appeal, plaintiffs concede that Missouri law requires insurers to charge their filed rates. But plaintiffs argue that the filed rate doctrine may not be applied to bar damage claims under federal civil rights statutes based upon the State's economic regulation of insurance rates. On this record, we agree with plaintiffs.

At its core, the filed rate doctrine has two components. It prohibits a regulated entity from discriminating between customers by charging a rate for its services other than the rate filed with the regulatory agency, and it preserves the authority and expertise of the rate-regulating agency by barring a court from enforcing the statute in a way that substitutes the court's judgment as to the reasonableness of a regulated rate. See *AT & T v. Central Office Tel., Inc.*, 524 U.S. 214, 221-23 (1998); *Arkansas La. Gas Co. v. Hall*, 453 U.S. 571 (1981); *Montana-Dakota Util. Co. v. Northwestern Pub. Serv. Co.*, 341 U.S. 246, 250-52 (1951).

In *Keogh*, the Supreme Court faced a somewhat different question, namely, whether a regulated entity's customers may recover treble damages under the federal antitrust laws because the rates, though approved by a federal rate-regulating agency, were the product of an illegal price fixing conspiracy. The Court noted that the regulatory agency's approval established the lawfulness of the filed rates. Therefore, the Court concluded, the antitrust [944] plaintiff could not recover damages because it had not been injured in its business or property within the meaning of the Sherman Act. 260 U.S. at 162-63. This is not an antitrust immunity, the Court later explained:

> The alleged collective activities of the defendants . . . were subject to scrutiny under the antitrust laws by the Government and to possible criminal sanctions or equitable relief. *Keogh* simply held that an award of treble damages is not an available remedy for a private shipper claiming that the rate submitted to, and approved by, the ICC was the product of an antitrust violation.

Square D Co. v. Niagara Frontier Tariff Bureau, Inc., 476 U.S. 409, 422 (1986). Having narrowly defined the scope of *Keogh* in this fashion, the Court in *Square D* declined to overrule this long-standing precedent.

In these cases, the district court applied the no-injury principle of *Keogh* to dismiss federal race discrimination claims because those claims challenge insurance premiums rates filed with a state regulatory agency. This ruling goes beyond the core of the filed rate doctrine, which simply allocates between a regulatory agency and the courts the authority to approve and enforce rates filed with the agency. Here, as in *Keogh* and *Square D*, the question is whether the agency's rate-regulating authority trumps the court's authority to enforce *a different statute*. Plaintiffs correctly argue that the Supreme Court in *Keogh* and *Square D* harmonized two federal statutes with competing purposes, the Sherman Act and the Interstate Commerce Act, whereas here the Supremacy Clause tips any legislative competition in favor of the federal anti-discrimination statutes. *City of Kirkwood v. Union Elec. Co.*, 671 F.2d 1173, 1178-79 n. 14 (8th Cir. 1982). Therefore, a decision that these federal claims are barred by the State's regulation of the defendants must be grounded in the language, remedies, and purposes of the *federal* statutes at issue.

Without question, this court and others have applied this aspect of the filed rate doctrine to bar federal RICO and antitrust claims seeking relief against utility rates filed with state regulatory agencies. *H.J. Inc. v. Northwestern Bell Tel. Co.*, 954 F.2d 485 (8th Cir.), cert. denied, 504 U.S. 957 (1992); see *Texas Commercial Energy v. TXU Energy, Inc.*, 413 F.3d 503 (5th Cir. 2005); *Wegoland Ltd. v. NYNEX Corp.*, 27 F.3d 17 (2d Cir. 1994); *Taffet v. Southern Co.*, 967 F.2d 1483 (11th Cir.) (en banc), cert. denied, 506 U.S. 1021 (1992). But RICO and the Sherman Act require a plaintiff to prove injury to "his business or property." 18 U.S.C. § 1964(c). Thus, the no-injury principle of *Keogh* applies to deprive a RICO or antitrust plaintiff of standing under federal law to challenge a filed rate that must be charged under state law. But standing to sue under federal anti-discrimination statutes such as the Fair Housing Act is far broader. See *Trafficante v. Metropolitan Life Ins. Co.*, 409 U.S. 205 (1972). If a defendant's pricing policies or practices were the product of unlawful race discrimination, plaintiffs who purchased homeowners insurance at the discriminatory rates have standing to seek [945] relief under these federal statutes even if the defendant was required by state law to charge its filed rates. Thus, as to this limited group of plaintiffs, the no-injury principle of *Keogh* and *H.J. Inc.* will not support an affirmance.

On appeal, beyond supporting the district court's flawed application of the *Keogh* no-injury principle, defendants simply argue at great length that federal courts should not interfere with the state regulatory regime by adjudicating claims that particular rates are the product of race discrimination. No doubt a ruling that rates are unlawfully discriminatory under federal law will have some impact on the state regulatory regime. But whether our jurisdiction to enforce the federal statutes should be set aside (or "reverse preempted") on this ground is a question for Congress, so the answer must be found in federal statutes. On this aspect of the inquiry, defendants and the district court are silent.

Congress addressed the extent to which enforcement of federal statutes may be permitted to impact state regulation of insurance in the McCarran-Ferguson Act, 15 U.S.C. §§ 1011-1015, enacted in response to the Supreme Court's ruling in *United States v. South-Eastern Underwriters Ass'n*, 322

U.S. 533 (1944), that insurance is interstate commerce under the Commerce Clause. Intending to leave the regulation of insurance primarily to the States, Congress provided, with exceptions not relevant here, that no federal statute "shall be construed to invalidate, impair, or supersede any law enacted by any State for the purpose of regulating the business of insurance . . . unless such [federal] Act specifically relates to the business of insurance." 15 U.S.C. § 1012(b). The Fair Housing Act, § 1981, and § 1982 do not specifically relate to the business of insurance, nor do they "invalidate" or "supersede" the Missouri laws regulating insurance. Thus, the question under the McCarran-Ferguson Act is whether enforcement of these federal statutes in the manner urged by plaintiffs would "impair" the State's regulation of insurance. State regulation is impaired only if the federal law "directly conflict[s] with state regulation," or if its application would "frustrate any declared state policy or interfere with a State's administrative regime." *Humana Inc., v. Forsyth*, 525 U.S. 299, 310 (1999).

Whether the adjudication of plaintiffs' pricing claims would impair Missouri's regime of insurance rate regulation under *Humana* is a fact-intensive issue that defendants did not raise in the district court or on appeal. The requisite level of interference is certainly more than possible. In holding that the filed rate doctrine barred RICO claims against a state-regulated electric utility, for example, Judge Tjoflat for the Eleventh Circuit summarized specific adverse impacts on the affected state regulatory regimes that might well constitute impairment for McCarran-Ferguson Act purposes. *Taffet*, 967 F.2d at 1491-92. Similarly, Judge Easterbrook in *NAACP v. American Family Mut. Ins. Co.*, 978 F.2d 287, 290-91 (7th Cir. 1992), *cert. denied*, 508 U.S. 907 (1993), and Judge Jones dissenting in *Dehoyos v. Allstate Corp.*, 345 F.3d 290, 300-02 (5th Cir. 2003), *cert. denied*, 541 U.S. 1010 (2004), gave powerful reasons why the relief requested in a disparate impact pricing claim under the Fair Housing Act could impair comprehensive state regulation of insurance rates. But a specific showing is needed. "The presence of a general regulatory scheme does not show that any particular state law would be invalidated, impaired or superseded by the application of the Fair Housing Act and the Civil Rights Acts." *Mackey v. Nationwide Ins.*, 724 F.2d 419, 421 (4th Cir. 1984).

Here, the record on appeal does not sufficiently delineate either the nature of plaintiffs' price discrimination claims, the specific relief they seek, or the extent of Missouri's insurance rate regulation to decide the McCarran-Ferguson Act impairment issue. We know defendants divide the State of Missouri into geographic rating territories and file different rating schedules for each territory, several of which are within Kansas City. We know that the Missouri administrative regime protects insureds from discriminatory pricing, see Mo.Rev.Stat. § 379.318.4, and that the agency may enforce compliance with this mandate in response to complaints by insureds, see Mo.Rev.Stat. §§ 379.348, 379.361. But we do not know whether insureds may bring an action in state court to challenge an insurance rate as discriminatory or unreasonable, nor do we know whether the Missouri statutes permit judicial review of the agency's determination of these issues. *Humana* teaches that the mere fact of overlapping complementary remedies under federal and state law does not constitute impairment for McCarran-Ferguson Act purposes. 525 U.S. at 313-14; see *Nationwide Mut. Ins. Co. v. Cisneros*, 52 F.3d 1351, 1363 (6th Cir. 1995), *cert. denied*, 516 U.S. 1140 (1996).

The Supreme Court has repeatedly emphasized "that federal courts have a strict duty to exercise the jurisdiction that is conferred upon them by Congress." *Quackenbush v. Allstate Ins. Co.*, 517 U.S. 706, 716 (1996). Here, rather than develop a record adequate to apply the federal statute that specifically addresses the problem, the McCarran-Ferguson Act, defendants brought Rule 12(b)(1) motions alleging that the filed rate doctrine deprives insureds of standing to assert race discrimination pricing claims under the Fair Housing Act and the Civil Rights Acts. The district court erred in invoking the judicially created filed rate doctrine to restrict Congress's broad grant of standing to seek judicial redress for race discrimination. That is the primary question before us regarding the pricing claims and the only question we decide.

III. Conclusion.

The following portions of the district court's final judgments are reversed and remanded for further proceedings not inconsistent with this opinion: in the Farmers action, the judgment dismissing the price discrimination claims of Kerry Butler and Kim Nickerson; in the American Family action, the judgment dismissing the price discrimination claims of plaintiffs Marva Saunders, Cynthia Canady, and Kerry Butler; in the Shelter action, the price discrimination claim of plaintiff Kerry Butler. In all other respects, the judgments are affirmed.

Add after the first paragraph in subsection 5 on Anti-Homeless Legislation on page 354:

This theory was adopted in *Jones v. City of Los Angeles*, 444 F.3d 1118 (9th Cir. 2006). The Ninth Circuit invalidated a Los Angeles "sit/lie" ordinance that made it illegal for any individual to sit, lie, or sleep on public streets and sidewalks. This ordinance is similar to other ordinances passed in many other cities, including Portland, Seattle, Tucson, Houston, and Philadelphia. The Ninth Circuit found that the Los Angeles ordinance was a violation of homeless individuals' Eighth Amendment rights against cruel and unusual punishment. The court found that the statute criminalized the status of being homeless, rather than a particular act. The court analyzed the Los Angeles ordinance based on the reasoning in the Supreme Court case of *Robinson v. California*, 370 U.S. 660 (1962). In *Robinson*, the Court invalidated a California law that criminalized addiction to narcotics. The Court reasoned that being addicted to narcotics is an illness, and "a state law which imprisons a person thus afflicted as a criminal, even though he has never touched any narcotic drug within the state or been guilty of any irregular behavior there, inflicts a cruel and unusual punishment in violation of the Fourteenth Amendment." *Robinson*, 370 U.S. at 667 (applying the Eighth Amendment to the states by incorporating its protections into the"liberty" safeguarded by the Fourteenth Amendment). The Ninth Circuit analogized the status of addiction to the status of being homeless and found that the Los Angeles ordinance was a violation of the Eighth Amendment.

CHAPTER 4

EMPLOYMENT DISCRIMINATION

Add the following sentence at the end of the last paragraph in Section A2 on page 378:

Also, state employment discrimination laws tend to have statutes of limitations that are more generous than the 180/300-day federal limitations period; see, e.g., *Haas v. Lockheed Martin Corp.*, 396 Md. 469, 914 A.2d 735 (2007) (discussing Md. Code, Art. 49B, § 42(b), which provides that discriminatory claims must be brought within two years of the alleged discriminatory act).

Add the following law review article just before the Oppenheimer article in the first paragraph on page 379:

Wendy Parker, *Lessons in Losing: Race Discrimination in Employment*, 81 Notre Dame L. Rev. 889 (2006);

Add the following sentence at the end of the first full paragraph on page 382:

For an interesting collection of cases and other materials that explore the sources of economic inequality (e.g., race, class, language, culture, and identity), see Emma Coleman Jordan and Angela Harris, *Economic Justice: Race, Gender, Identity and Economics* (2005).

Replace the discussion concerning the jurisdictional status of the 15-employee threshold that appears in the bottom quarter of Note 3 on page 388 with the following new Note 3.1:

3.1. Resolving a long-running split among the circuit courts, a unanimous Supreme Court, in *Arbaugh v. Y & H Corp.*, 126 S. Ct. 1235 (2006), ruled that the 15-employee numerical threshold is substantive rather than jurisdictional. The procedural implications of the Court's ruling are quite significant. First, by holding that the numerosity threshold is an element of the plaintiff's Title VII claim rather than a matter of the district court's subject matter jurisdiction, the Court, in effect, is saying that the dismissal of the case on such grounds is based on Fed. F. Civ. Proc. 12(b)(6) ("failure to state a claim for which relief can be granted") rather than on Fed. F. Civ. Pro. 12(b)(1) ("lack of jurisdiction over the subject matter"). This means that the "first appearance rule" applies (remember civil procedure). Consequently, the defendant must move for dismissal at the time of its first appearance in the district court. Rule 12(b)(1), but not Rule 12(b)(6), motions can be raised at any time, even after entry of the judgement in favor of the plaintiff (see Rule 12(h)(3). The defendant in *Arbaugh* waited until after the entry of judgment in favor of the plaintiff to move for dismissal. Not lost on the Court was the "unfairness" and "waste of judicial resources" that can result from nullifying a decision rendered on the merits, when, the defendant is allowed to raise the jurisdictional challenge so late in the litigation. Second, state supplemental claims can survive a dismissal of federal question claim, like the Title VII, when the dismissal is based on grounds *other than* subject matter jurisdiction (see 29 U.S.C. § 1367). Thus, in *Arbaugh*, plaintiff's state-related claims would have survived dismissal of her Title VII sexual harassment claim had the Court upheld the motion for dismissal been timely filed. Interestingly, the Court noted that Congress could make the numerosity requirement jurisdictional by simply amending Title VII and placing the requirement in the statute's jurisdictional section.

Add the following sentence to the end of the next-to-last paragraph on page 390:

Should pay-discrimination claims be treated under the *Ricks* rule or closer to § 706(e)(2)? In *Ledbetter v. Goodyear Tire & Rubber Co.*, 2007 U.S. LEXIS 6295, the Supreme Court, in a 5-4 opinion written by Justice Alito, adopted the *Ricks* rule for pay-discrimination claims, holding that Title VII's limitation period begins when a discriminatory pay decision is made and communicated to the employee. In dissent, Justice Ginsburg argued that the Court's insistence upon an immediate response to a discriminatory pay decision (180 days in nondeferral states, 300 days in deferral states) simply ignores the real world of pay discrimination. Pay discrimination typically occurs in small increments rather than in singular discrete acts: cause for suspicion that discrimination is at work occurs over time, and comparable pay information is often hidden from the employee. For example, in *Ledbetter*, the plaintiff was initially pay the same salary as her male co-workers, but overtime a substantial pay differential grew as she received smaller raises. At the time of her lawsuit, plaintiff's salary fell by 40 percent. Title VII's short statute of limitations is one of the reasons many race-based employment discrimination cases are brought under an alternative civil rights statute, Section 1981. This provision would not have helped the plaintiff in *Ledbetter*, however, because it only applies to race-based claims; it does not apply to gender-based claims. See Section E1, infra.

Replace *Gastineau v. Fleet Mortg. Corp.* in the middle of the page on page 398 with the following cases:

Walsh v. Nev. Dep't of Human Res., 471 F.3d 1033 (9th Cir. 2006) (individuals are not personally liable for damages under Title VII or ADA); *Dearth v. Collins*, 441 F. 3d 931 (11th Cir. 2006) (court will not "pierce the corporate veil" to find individual liability pursuant to the "alter ego" doctrine); *Worth v. Tyler*, 276 F.3d 249 (7th Cir 2001)(same).

Add the following sentences at the end of the last paragraph on page 400:

Should Title VII prohibit "trait discrimination," which is discrimination based on traits that are statistically or culturally associated with a particular racial group? Should it matter whether the trait in question is arguably job-related (e.g., the applicant lacks the type of appearance that makes the customers of a certain restaurant feel "comfortable") or not (e.g., the employer just does not like a certain type of look)? See Kimberly A. Yuracko, *Trait Discrimination as Race Discrimination: An Argument About Assimilation*, 74 Geo. Wash. L. Rev. 365 (2006).

Replace *Sitar v. Indiana Dept. of Transportation* in the last line on page 403 with the following citation:

See, e.g., *Rochon v. Gonzales*, 438 F3d1211 (D.C. Cir. 2006) (retaliation claim against Executive Branch of federal government).

Add the following new case after the last paragraph on page 403:

Burlington Northern & Santa Fe Railway Co. v. White

2006 U.S. LEXIS 4895 (2006)

BREYER, J., delivered the opinion of the Court, in which ROBERTS, C. J., and STEVENS, SCALIA, KENNEDY, SOUTER, THOMAS, and GINSBURG, JJ., joined. ALITO, J., filed an opinion concurring in the judgment.

JUSTICE BREYER delivered the opinion of the Court.

Title VII of the Civil Rights Act of 1964 forbids employment discrimination against "any individual" based on that individual's "race, color, religion, sex, or national origin." Pub. L. 88-352, § 704, 78 Stat. 257, as amended, *42 U.S.C. § 2000e-2(a)*. A separate section of the Act -- its anti-retaliation provision -- forbids an employer from "discriminating against" an employee or job applicant because that individual "opposed any practice" made unlawful by Title VII or "made a charge, testified, assisted, or participated in" a Title VII proceeding or investigation. *§ 2000e-3(a).*

The Courts of Appeals have come to different conclusions about the scope of the Act's anti-retaliation provision, particularly the reach of its phrase "discriminate against." Does that provision confine actionable retaliation to activity that affects the terms and conditions of employment? And how harmful must the adverse actions be to fall within its scope?

We conclude that the anti-retaliation provision does not confine the actions and harms it forbids to those that are related to employment or occur at the workplace. We also conclude that the provision covers those (and only those) employer actions that would have been materially adverse to a reasonable employee or job applicant. In the present context that means that the employer's actions must be harmful to the point that they could well dissuade a reasonable worker from making or supporting a charge of discrimination.

I

A

This case arises out of actions that supervisors at petitioner Burlington Northern & Santa Fe Railway Company took against respondent Sheila White, the only woman working in the Maintenance of Way department at Burlington's Tennessee Yard. In June 1997, Burlington's roadmaster, Marvin Brown, interviewed White and expressed interest in her previous experience operating forklifts. Burlington hired White as a "track laborer," a job that involves removing and replacing track components, transporting track material, cutting brush, and clearing litter and cargo spillage from the right-of-way. Soon after White arrived on the job, a co-worker who had previously operated the forklift chose to assume other responsibilities. Brown immediately assigned White to operate the forklift. While she also performed some of the other track laborer tasks, operating the forklift was White's primary responsibility.

In September 1997, White complained to Burlington officials that her immediate supervisor, Bill Joiner, had repeatedly told her that women should not be working in the Maintenance of Way department. Joiner, White said, had also made insulting and inappropriate remarks to her in front of her male colleagues. After an internal investigation, Burlington suspended Joiner for 10 days and ordered him to attend a sexual-harassment training session.

On September 26, Brown told White about Joiner's discipline. At the same time, he told White that he was removing her from forklift duty and assigning her to perform only standard track laborer tasks. Brown explained that the reassignment reflected co-worker's complaints that, in fairness, a "'more senior man'" should have the "less arduous and cleaner job" of forklift operator. *364 F.3d 789, 792 (CA6 2004)* (case below).

On October 10, White filed a complaint with the Equal Employment Opportunity Commission (EEOC or Commission). She claimed that the reassignment of her duties amounted to unlawful gender-based discrimination and retaliation for her having earlier complained about Joiner. In early December, White filed a second retaliation charge with the Commission, claiming that Brown had placed her under surveillance and was monitoring her daily activities. That charge was mailed to Brown on December 8.

A few days later, White and her immediate supervisor, Percy Sharkey, disagreed about which truck should transport White from one location to another. The specific facts of the disagreement are in dispute, but the upshot is that Sharkey told Brown later that afternoon that White had been insubordinate. Brown immediately suspended White without pay. White invoked internal grievance procedures. Those procedures led Burlington to conclude that White had *not* been insubordinate. Burlington reinstated White to her position and awarded her backpay for the 37 days she was suspended. White filed an additional retaliation charge with the EEOC based on the suspension.

B

After exhausting administrative remedies, White filed this Title VII action against Burlington in federal court. As relevant here, she claimed that Burlington's actions -- (1) changing her job responsibilities, and (2) suspending her for 37 days without pay -- amounted to unlawful retaliation in violation of Title VII. *§ 2000e-3(a)*. A jury found in White's favor on both of these claims. It awarded her $ 43,500 in compensatory damages, including $ 3,250 in medical expenses. . . .

Initially, a divided Sixth Circuit panel reversed the judgment and found in Burlington's favor on the retaliation claims. *310 F.3d 443 (2002)*. The full Court of Appeals vacated the panel's decision, however, and heard the matter en banc. The court then affirmed the District Court's judgment in White's favor on both retaliation claims. While all members of the en banc court voted to uphold the District Court's judgment, they differed as to the proper standard to apply. Compare *364 F.3d at 795-800*, with *id., at 809* (Clay, J., concurring).

II

Title VII's anti-retaliation provision forbids employer actions that "discriminate against" an employee (or job applicant) because he has "opposed" a practice that Title VII forbids or has "made a charge, testified, assisted, or participated in" a Title VII "investigation, proceeding, or hearing." *§ 2000e-3(a)*. No one doubts that the term "discriminate against" refers to distinctions or differences in treatment that injure protected individuals. See *Jackson v. Birmingham Bd. of Ed., 544 U.S. 167, 174 (2005)*; *Price Waterhouse v. Hopkins, 490 U.S. 228, 244 (1989)* (plurality opinion); see also 4 Oxford English Dictionary 758 (2d ed. 1989) (def. 3b). But different Circuits have come to different conclusions about whether the challenged action has to be employment or workplace related and about how harmful that action must be to constitute retaliation.

Some Circuits have insisted upon a close relationship between the retaliatory action and employment. The Sixth Circuit majority in this case, for example, said that a plaintiff must show an "adverse employment action," which it defined as a "materially adverse change in the terms and conditions" of employment. *364 F.3d at 795* (internal quotation marks omitted). The Sixth Circuit has thus joined those Courts of Appeals that apply the same standard for retaliation that they apply to a substantive discrimination offense, holding that the challenged action must "result in an adverse effect on the 'terms, conditions, or benefits' of employment." *Von Gunten v. Maryland, 243 F.3d 858, 866*

(CA4 2001); see *Robinson v. Pittsburgh, 120 F.3d 1286, 1300 (CA3 1997).* The Fifth and the Eighth Circuits have adopted a more restrictive approach. They employ an "ultimate employment decision" standard, which limits actionable retaliatory conduct to acts "'such as hiring, granting leave, discharging, promoting, and compensating.'" *Mattern v. Eastman Kodak Co., 104 F.3d 702, 707 (CA5 1997)*; see *Manning v. Metropolitan Life Ins. Co., 127 F.3d 686, 692 (CA8 1997).*

Other Circuits have not so limited the scope of the provision. The Seventh and the District of Columbia Circuits have said that the plaintiff must show that the "employer's challenged action would have been material to a reasonable employee," which in contexts like the present one means that it would likely have "dissuaded a reasonable worker from making or supporting a charge of discrimination." *Washington v. Ill. Dep't of Revenue, 420 F.3d 658, 662 (CA7 2005)*; see *Rochon v. Gonzales, 438 F.3d 1211, 1217-1218 (CADC 2006).* And the Ninth Circuit, following EEOC guidance, has said that the plaintiff must simply establish "'adverse treatment that is based on a retaliatory motive and is reasonably likely to deter the charging party or others from engaging in protected activity.'" *Ray v. Henderson, 217 F.3d 1234, 1242-1243 (CA9 2000).* The concurring judges below would have applied this last mentioned standard. *364 F.3d at 809* (opinion of Clay, J.).

We granted certiorari to resolve this disagreement. To do so requires us to decide whether Title VII's anti-retaliation provision forbids only those employer actions and resulting harms that are related to employment or the workplace. And we must characterize how harmful an act of retaliatory discrimination must be in order to fall within the provision's scope.

A

Petitioner and the Solicitor General both argue that the Sixth Circuit is correct to require a link between the challenged retaliatory action and the terms, conditions, or status of employment. They note that Title VII's substantive anti-discrimination provision protects an individual only from employment-related discrimination. They add that the anti-retaliation provision should be read *in pari materia* with the anti-discrimination provision. And they conclude that the employer actions prohibited by the anti-retaliation provision should similarly be limited to conduct that "affects the employee's 'compensation, terms, conditions, or privileges of employment.'" Brief for United States as *Amicus Curiae* 13 (quoting *§ 2000e-2(a)(1)*); see Brief for Petitioner 13 (same).

We cannot agree. The language of the substantive provision differs from that of the anti-retaliation provision in important ways. *Section 703(a)* sets forth Title VII's core anti-discrimination provision in the following terms:

> "It shall be an unlawful employment practice for an employer --
>
> "(1) *to fail or refuse to hire or to discharge* any individual, or otherwise to discriminate against any individual *with respect to his compensation, terms, conditions, or privileges of employment*, because of such individual's race, color, religion, sex, or national origin; or

"(2) to limit, segregate, or classify his employees or applicants for employment in any way *which would deprive or tend to deprive any individual of employment opportunities or otherwise adversely affect his status as an employee*, because of such individual's race, color, religion, sex, or national origin." *§ 2000e-2(a)* (emphasis added).

Section 704(a) sets forth Title VII's anti-retaliation provision in the following terms:

"It shall be an unlawful employment practice for an employer *to discriminate against* any of his employees or applicants for employment . . . because he has opposed any practice made an unlawful employment practice by this subchapter, or because he has made a charge, testified, assisted, or participated in any manner in an investigation, proceeding, or hearing under this subchapter." *§ 2000e-3(a)* (emphasis added).

The underscored words in the substantive provision -- "hire," "discharge," "compensation, terms, conditions, or privileges of employment," "employment opportunities," and "status as an employee" -- explicitly limit the scope of that provision to actions that affect employment or alter the conditions of the workplace. No such limiting words appear in the anti-retaliation provision. Given these linguistic differences, the question here is not whether identical or similar words should be read *in pari materia* to mean the same thing. See, *e.g.*, *Pasquantino v. United States, 544 U.S. 349, 355, n. 2 (2005)*. . . . Rather, the question is whether Congress intended its different words to make a legal difference. We normally presume that, where words differ as they differ here, "'Congress acts intentionally and purposely in the disparate inclusion or exclusion.'" *Russello v. United States, 464 U.S. 16, 23 (1983)*.

There is strong reason to believe that Congress intended the differences that its language suggests, for the two provisions differ not only in language but in purpose as well. The anti-discrimination provision seeks a workplace where individuals are not discriminated against because of their racial, ethnic, religious, or gender-based status. See *McDonnell Douglas Corp. v. Green, 411 U.S. 792, 800-801 (1973)*. The anti-retaliation provision seeks to secure that primary objective by preventing an employer from interfering (through retaliation) with an employee's efforts to secure or advance enforcement of the Act's basic guarantees. The substantive provision seeks to prevent injury to individuals based on who they are, *i.e.*, their status. The anti-retaliation provision seeks to prevent harm to individuals based on what they do, *i.e.*, their conduct.

To secure the first objective, Congress did not need to prohibit anything other than employment-related discrimination. The substantive provision's basic objective of "equality of employment opportunities" and the elimination of practices that tend to bring about "stratified job environments," *id., at 800*, would be achieved were all employment-related discrimination miraculously eliminated.

But one cannot secure the second objective by focusing only upon employer actions and harm that concern employment and the workplace. Were all such actions and harms eliminated, the anti-retaliation provision's objective would *not* be achieved. An employer can effectively retaliate against an employee by taking actions not directly related to his employment or by causing him harm *outside* the workplace. See, *e.g.*, *Rochon v. Gonzales, 438 F.3d at 1213* (FBI retaliation against employee "took the form of the FBI's refusal, contrary to policy, to investigate death threats a federal prisoner made against [the agent] and his wife"); *Berry v. Stevinson Chevrolet, 74 F.3d 980, 984, 986 (CA10 1996)* (finding actionable retaliation where employer filed false criminal charges against former employee who complained about discrimination). A provision limited to employment-related actions would not deter the many forms that effective retaliation can take. Hence, such a limited construction would fail to fully achieve the anti-retaliation provision's "primary purpose," namely, "maintaining unfettered access to statutory remedial mechanisms." *Robinson v. Shell Oil Co., 519 U.S. 337, 346 (1997).*

Thus, purpose reinforces what language already indicates, namely, that the anti-retaliation provision, unlike the substantive provision, is not limited to discriminatory actions that affect the terms and conditions of employment. . . .

Our precedent does not compel a contrary conclusion. Indeed, we have found no case in this Court that offers petitioner or the United States significant support. *Burlington Industries, Inc. v. Ellerth, 524 U.S. 742 (1998)*, as petitioner notes, speaks of a Title VII requirement that violations involve "tangible employment action" such as "hiring, firing, failing to promote, reassignment with significantly different responsibilities, or a decision causing a significant change in benefits." *Id., at 761*. But *Ellerth* does so only to "identify a class of [hostile work environment] cases" in which an employer should be held vicariously liable (without an affirmative defense) for the acts of supervisors. *Id., at 760. . . . Ellerth* did not discuss the scope of the general anti-discrimination provision. See *524 U.S., at 761 . . . .* And *Ellerth* did not mention Title VII's anti-retaliation provision at all. At most, *Ellerth* sets forth a standard that petitioner and the Solicitor General believe the anti-retaliation provision ought to contain. But it does not compel acceptance of their view.

Nor can we find significant support for their view in the EEOC's interpretations of the provision. We concede that the EEOC stated in its 1991 and 1988 Compliance Manuals that the anti-retaliation provision is limited to "adverse employment-related action." 2 EEOC Compliance Manual § 614.1(d), p. 614-5 (1991) (hereinafter EEOC 1991 Manual); EEOC Compliance Manual § 614.1(d), p. 614-5 (1988) (hereinafter EEOC 1988 Manual). But in those same manuals the EEOC lists the "essential elements" of a retaliation claim along with language suggesting a broader interpretation. EEOC 1991 Manual § 614.3(d), pp. 614-8 to 614-9 (complainant must show "that (s)he was in some manner subjected to adverse treatment by the respondent because of the protest or opposition"); EEOC 1988 Manual § 614.3(d), pp. 614-8 to 614-9 (same).

Moreover, both before and after publication of the 1991 and 1988 manuals, the EEOC similarly expressed a broad interpretation of the anti-retaliation provision. Compare EEOC Interpretive

Manual, Reference Manual to Title VII Law for Compliance Personnel § 491.2 (1972) (hereinafter 1972 Reference Manual) (*§ 704(a)* "is intended to provide 'exceptionally broad protection' for protestors of discriminatory employment practices"), with 2 EEOC Compliance Manual § 8, p. 8-13 (1998) (hereinafter EEOC 1998 Manual), available at http://www.eeoc.gov/policy/docs/ retal.html (as visited June 20, 2006, and available in Clerk of Court's case file) (*§ 704(a)* "prohibits any adverse treatment that is based on a retaliatory motive and is reasonably likely to deter the charging party or others from engaging in protected activity"). . . .

Finally, we do not accept the petitioner's and Solicitor General's view that it is "anomalous" to read the statute to provide broader protection for victims of retaliation than for those whom Title VII primarily seeks to protect, namely, victims of race-based, ethnic-based, religion-based, or gender-based discrimination. Brief for Petitioner 17; Brief for United States as *Amicus Curiae* 14-15. Congress has provided similar kinds of protection from retaliation in comparable statutes without any judicial suggestion that those provisions are limited to the conduct prohibited by the primary substantive provisions. The National Labor Relations Act, to which this Court has "drawn analogies . . . in other Title VII contexts," *Hishon v. King & Spalding, 467 U.S. 69, 76, n. 8 (1984)*, provides an illustrative example. Compare *29 U.S.C. § 158(a)(3)* (substantive provision prohibiting employer "discrimination in regard to . . . any term or condition of employment to encourage or discourage membership in any labor organization") with *§ 158(a)(4)* (retaliation provision making it unlawful for an employer to "discharge or otherwise discriminate against an employee because he has filed charges or given testimony under this subchapter"); see also. . . . *NLRB v. Scrivener, 405 U.S. 117, 121-122 (1972)* (purpose of the anti-retaliation provision is to ensure that employees are "'completely free from coercion against reporting'" unlawful practices).

In any event, as we have explained, differences in the purpose of the two provisions remove any perceived "anomaly," for they justify this difference of interpretation. See *supra*, at 8-9. Title VII depends for its enforcement upon the cooperation of employees who are willing to file complaints and act as witnesses. "Plainly, effective enforcement could thus only be expected if employees felt free to approach officials with their grievances." *Mitchell v. Robert DeMario Jewelry, Inc., 361 U.S. 288, 292 (1960)*. Interpreting the anti-retaliation provision to provide broad protection from retaliation helps assure the cooperation upon which accomplishment of the Act's primary objective depends.

For these reasons, we conclude that Title VII's substantive provision and its anti-retaliation provision are not coterminous. The scope of the anti-retaliation provision extends beyond workplace-related or employment-related retaliatory acts and harm. We therefore reject the standards applied in the Courts of Appeals that have treated the anti-retaliation provision as forbidding the same conduct prohibited by the anti-discrimination provision and that have limited actionable retaliation to so-called "ultimate employment decisions." See *supra*, at 5.

B

The anti-retaliation provision protects an individual not from all retaliation, but from retaliation that produces an injury or harm. As we have explained, the Courts of Appeals have used differing language to describe the level of seriousness to which this harm must rise before it becomes actionable retaliation. We agree with the formulation set forth by the Seventh and the District of Columbia Circuits. In our view, a plaintiff must show that a reasonable employee would have found the challenged action materially adverse, "which in this context means it well might have 'dissuaded a reasonable worker from making or supporting a charge of discrimination.'" *Rochon, 438 F.3d at 1219* (quoting *Washington, 420 F.3d at 662*).

We speak of *material* adversity because we believe it is important to separate significant from trivial harms. Title VII, we have said, does not set forth "a general civility code for the American workplace." *Oncale v. Sundowner Offshore Services, Inc., 523 U.S. 75, 80 (1998)* . . . An employee's decision to report discriminatory behavior cannot immunize that employee from those petty slights or minor annoyances that often take place at work and that all employees experience. See 1 B. Lindemann & P. Grossman, Employment Discrimination Law 669 (3d ed. 1996) (noting that "courts have held that personality conflicts at work that generate antipathy" and "'snubbing' by supervisors and co-workers" are not actionable under *§ 704(a)*). The anti-retaliation provision seeks to prevent employer interference with "unfettered access" to Title VII's remedial mechanisms. *Robinson, 519 U.S., at 346.* It does so by prohibiting employer actions that are likely "to deter victims of discrimination from complaining to the EEOC," the courts, and their employers. *Ibid.* And normally petty slights, minor annoyances, and simple lack of good manners will not create such deterrence. See 2 EEOC 1998 Manual § 8, p. 8-13.

We refer to reactions of a *reasonable* employee because we believe that the provision's standard for judging harm must be objective. An objective standard is judicially administrable. It avoids the uncertainties and unfair discrepancies that can plague a judicial effort to determine a plaintiff's unusual subjective feelings. We have emphasized the need for objective standards in other Title VII contexts, and those same concerns animate our decision here. See, *e.g.*, *Suders, 542 U.S., at 141* (constructive discharge doctrine); *Harris v. Forklift Systems, Inc., 510 U.S. 17, 21 (1993)* (hostile work environment doctrine).

We phrase the standard in general terms because the significance of any given act of retaliation will often depend upon the particular circumstances. Context matters. "The real social impact of workplace behavior often depends on a constellation of surrounding circumstances, expectations, and relationships which are not fully captured by a simple recitation of the words used or the physical acts performed." *Oncale, supra, at 81-82.* A schedule change in an employee's work schedule may make little difference to many workers, but may matter enormously to a young mother with school age children. Cf., *e.g.*, *Washington, supra, at 662* (finding flex-time schedule critical to employee with disabled child). A supervisor's refusal to invite an employee to lunch is normally trivial, a nonactionable petty slight. But to retaliate by excluding an employee from a weekly training lunch that contributes significantly to the employee's professional advancement might well deter a reasonable employee from complaining about discrimination. See 2 EEOC 1998 Manual § 8, p. 8-14. Hence, a legal standard that speaks in general terms rather than specific prohibited acts is preferable, for an "act that would be immaterial in some situations is material in others." *Washington, supra, at 661.*

Finally, we note that contrary to the claim of the concurrence, this standard does *not* require a reviewing court or jury to consider "the nature of the discrimination that led to the filing of the charge." *Post*, at 6 (ALITO, J., concurring in judgment). Rather, the standard is tied to the challenged retaliatory act, not the underlying conduct that forms the basis of the Title VII complaint. By focusing on the materiality of the challenged action and the perspective of a reasonable person in the plaintiff's position, we believe this standard will screen out trivial conduct while effectively capturing those acts that are likely to dissuade employees from complaining or assisting in complaints about discrimination.

III

Applying this standard to the facts of this case, we believe that there was a sufficient evidentiary basis to support the jury's verdict on White's retaliation claim. See *Reeves v. Sanderson Plumbing Products, Inc., 530 U.S. 133, 150-151 (2000).* The jury found that two of Burlington's actions amounted to retaliation: the reassignment of White from forklift duty to standard track laborer tasks and the 37-day suspension without pay.

Burlington does not question the jury's determination that the motivation for these acts was retaliatory. But it does question the statutory significance of the harm these acts caused. . . .

First, Burlington argues that a reassignment of duties cannot constitute retaliatory discrimination where, as here, both the former and present duties fall within the same job description. Brief for Petitioner 24-25. We do not see why that is so. Almost every job category involves some responsibilities and duties that are less desirable than others. Common sense suggests that one good way to discourage an employee such as White from bringing discrimination charges would be to insist that she spend more time performing the more arduous duties and less time performing those that are easier or more agreeable. That is presumably why the EEOC has consistently found "retaliatory work assignments" to be a classic and "widely recognized" example of "forbidden retaliation." 2 EEOC 1991 Manual § 614.7, pp. 614-31 to 614-32 . . . . *EEOC Dec. No. 74-77, 1974 EEOC LEXIS 2, 1974 WL 3847, *4 (Jan. 18, 1974)* ("Employers have been enjoined" under Title VII "from imposing unpleasant work assignments upon an employee for filing charges").

To be sure, reassignment of job duties is not automatically actionable. Whether a particular reassignment is materially adverse depends upon the circumstances of the particular case, and "should be judged from the perspective of a reasonable person in the plaintiff's position, considering 'all the circumstances.'" *Oncale, 523 U.S., at 81.* But here, the jury had before it considerable evidence that the track labor duties were "by all accounts more arduous and dirtier"; that the "forklift operator position required more qualifications, which is an indication of prestige"; and that "the forklift operator position was objectively considered a better job and the male employees resented White for occupying it." *364 F.3d at 803* (internal quotation marks omitted). Based on this record, a jury could reasonably conclude that the reassignment of responsibilities would have been materially adverse to a reasonable employee.

Second, Burlington argues that the 37-day suspension without pay lacked statutory significance because Burlington ultimately reinstated White with backpay. Burlington says that "it defies reason to believe that Congress would have considered a rescinded investigatory suspension with full back pay" to be unlawful, particularly because Title VII, throughout much of its history, provided no relief in an equitable action for victims in White's position. Brief for Petitioner 36.

We do not find Burlington's last mentioned reference to the nature of Title VII's remedies convincing. After all, throughout its history, Title VII has provided for injunctions to "bar like discrimination in the future," *Albemarle Paper Co. v. Moody, 422 U.S. 405, 418 (1975)* (internal quotation marks omitted), an important form of relief. Pub. L. 88-352, § 706(g), 78 Stat. 261, as amended, *42 U.S.C. § 2000e-5(g)*. And we have no reason to believe that a court could not have issued an injunction where an employer suspended an employee for retaliatory purposes, even if that employer later provided backpay. In any event, Congress amended Title VII in 1991 to permit victims of intentional discrimination to recover compensatory (as White received here) and punitive damages, concluding that the additional remedies were necessary to "'help make victims whole.'" *West v. Gibson, 527 U.S. 212, 219 (1999)* (quoting H. R. Rep. No. 102-40, pt. 1, pp. 64-65 (1991)). . . . We would undermine the significance of that congressional judgment were we to conclude that employers could avoid liability in these circumstances.

Neither do we find convincing any claim of insufficient evidence. White did receive backpay. But White and her family had to live for 37 days without income. They did not know during that time whether or when White could return to work. Many reasonable employees would find a month without a paycheck to be a serious hardship. And White described to the jury the physical and emotional hardship that 37 days of having "no income, no money" in fact caused. 1 Tr. 154 ("That was the worst Christmas I had out of my life. No income, no money, and that made all of us feel bad. . . . I got very depressed"). Indeed, she obtained medical treatment for her emotional distress. A reasonable employee facing the choice between retaining her job (and paycheck) and filing a discrimination complaint might well choose the former. That is to say, an indefinite suspension without pay could well act as a deterrent, even if the suspended employee eventually received backpay. . . . . Thus, the jury's conclusion that the 37-day suspension without pay was materially adverse was a reasonable one.

IV

For these reasons, the judgment of the Court of Appeals is affirmed.

It is so ordered.

JUSTICE ALITO, concurring in the judgment.

I concur in the judgment, but I disagree with the majority's interpretation of the antiretaliation provision of Title VII of the Civil Rights Act of 1964, 78 Stat. 257, § 704(a), as amended, *42 U.S.C.*

§ 2000e-3(a). The majority's interpretation has no basis in the statutory language and will, I fear, lead to practical problems.

I

Two provisions of Title VII are important here. *Section 703(a)* prohibits a broad range of discriminatory employment practices. Among other things, *§ 703(a)* makes it unlawful for an employer "*to discriminate against* any individual with respect to his compensation, terms, conditions, or privileges of employment, because of such individual's race, color, religion, sex, or national origin." *42 U.S.C. § 2000e-2(a)(1)* (emphasis added).

A complementary and closely related provision, *§ 704(a)*, makes it unlawful to "discriminate against" an employee for retaliatory purposes. . . .

In this case, we must ascertain the meaning of the term "discriminate" in *§ 704(a)*. Two possible interpretations are suggested by the language of *§ § 703(a)* and *704(a)*.

The first is the interpretation that immediately springs to mind if *§ 704(a)* is read by itself -- *i.e.*, that the term "discriminate" in *§ 704(a)* means what the term literally means, to treat differently. Respondent staunchly defends this interpretation, which the majority does not embrace, but this interpretation presents problems that are at least sufficient to raise doubts about its correctness. Respondent's interpretation makes *§ 703(a)* narrower in scope than *§ 704(a)* and thus implies that the persons whom Title VII is principally designed to protect -- victims of discrimination based on race, color, sex, national origin, or religion -- receive less protection than victims of retaliation. In addition, respondent's interpretation "makes a federal case" out of any small difference in the way an employee who has engaged in protected conduct is treated. On respondent's view, a retaliation claim must go to the jury if the employee creates a genuine issue on such questions as whether the employee was given any more or less work than others, was subjected to any more or less supervision, or was treated in a somewhat less friendly manner because of his protected activity. . . .

The other plausible interpretation, and the one I favor, reads *§ § 703(a)* and *704(a)* together. Under this reading, "discrimination" under *§ 704(a)* means the discriminatory acts reached by *§ 703(a)* -- chiefly, discrimination "with respect to . . . compensation, terms, conditions, or privileges of employment." This is not, admittedly, the most straightforward reading of the bare language of *§ 704(a)*, but it is a reasonable reading that harmonizes *§ § 703(a)* and *704(a)*. It also provides an objective standard that permits insignificant claims to be weeded out at the summary judgment stage, while providing ample protection for employees who are subjected to real retaliation.

The Courts of Appeals that have interpreted *§ 704(a)* in this way state that it requires a materially adverse employment action. See, *e.g.*, *Von Gunten v. Maryland, 243 F.3d 858, 865 (CA4 2001)*. . . . In *Burlington Industries, Inc. v. Ellerth, 524 U.S. 742, 761-762 (1998)*, we "imported" this test for use in a different context -- to define the term "tangible employment action," a concept we used to limit an employer's liability for harassment carried out by its supervisors. We explained that "[a] tangible employment action constitutes a significant change in employment status, such as hiring, firing, failing to promote, reassignment with significantly different responsibilities, or a decision causing a significant change in benefits." *Id., at 761.*

II

The majority does not adopt either of the two interpretations noted above. In Part II-A of its opinion, the majority criticizes the interpretation that harmonizes *§ § 703(a)* and *704(a)* as not sufficiently faithful to the language of *§ 704(a)*. Although we found the materially adverse employment action test worthy of "importation" in *Ellerth*, the majority now argues that this test is too narrow because it permits employers to take retaliatory measures outside the workplace. *Ante*, at 8-9 . . . . But the majority's concern is misplaced.

First, an employer who wishes to retaliate against an employee for engaging in protected conduct is much more likely to do so on the job. There are far more opportunities for retaliation in that setting, and many forms of retaliation off the job constitute crimes and are therefore especially risky.

Second, the materially adverse employment action test is not limited to on-the-job retaliation, as *Rochon*, one of the cases cited by the majority, illustrates. There, a Federal Bureau of Investigation agent claimed that the Bureau had retaliated against him by failing to provide the off-duty security that would otherwise have been furnished. See *438 F.3d at 1213-1214*. But, for an FBI agent whose life may be threatened during off-duty hours, providing security easily qualifies as a term, condition, or privilege of employment. Certainly, if the FBI had a policy of denying protection to agents of a particular race, such discrimination would be actionable under *§ 703(a)*.

But in Part II-B, rather than adopting the more literal interpretation based on the language of *§ 704(a)* alone, the majority instead puts that language aside and adopts a third interpretation -- one that has no grounding in the statutory language. According to the majority, *§ 704(a)* does not reach all retaliatory differences in treatment but only those retaliatory acts that "well might have dissuaded a reasonable worker from making or supporting a charge of discrimination." *Ante*, at 13 (internal quotation marks omitted).

I see no sound basis for this test. The language of *§ 704(a)*, which employs the unadorned term "discriminate," does not support this test. The unstated premise of the majority's reasoning seems to be that *§ 704(a)*'s only purpose is to prevent employers from taking those actions that are likely to stop employees from complaining about discrimination, but this unstated premise is unfounded. While surely *one of the purposes* of *§ 704(a)* is to prevent employers from engaging in retaliatory measures that dissuade employees from engaging in protected conduct, there is no reason to suppose that this is *§ 704(a)*'s only purpose. Indeed, the majority itself identifies another purpose of the antiretaliation provision: "to prevent harm to individuals" who assert their rights. *Ante*, at 8. Under the majority's test, however, employer conduct that causes harm to an employee is permitted so long as the employer conduct is not so severe as to dissuade a reasonable employee from making or supporting a charge of discrimination.

III

The practical consequences of the test that the majority adopts strongly suggest that this test is not what Congress intended.

First, the majority's test leads logically to perverse results. Under the majority's test, *§ 704(a)* reaches retaliation that well might dissuade an employee from making or supporting "a charge of discrimination." *Ante*, at 13 (internal quotation marks omitted). I take it that the phrase "*a* charge of discrimination" means the particular charge that the employee in question filed, and if that is the proper interpretation, the nature of the discrimination that led to the filing of the charge must be taken into account in applying *§ 704(a)*. Specifically, the majority's interpretation logically implies that the degree of protection afforded to a victim of retaliation is inversely proportional to the severity of the original act of discrimination that prompted the retaliation. A reasonable employee who is subjected to the most severe discrimination will not easily be dissuaded from filing a charge by the threat of retaliation; the costs of filing the charge, including possible retaliation, will have to be great to outweigh the benefits, such as preventing the continuation of the discrimination in the future and obtaining damages and other relief for past discrimination. Because the possibility of relatively severe retaliation will not easily dissuade this employee, the employer will be able to engage in relatively severe retaliation without incurring liability under *§ 704(a)*. On the other hand, an employee who is subjected to a much milder form of discrimination will be much more easily dissuaded. For this employee, the costs of complaining, including possible retaliation, will not have to be great to outweigh the lesser benefits that might be obtained by filing a charge. These topsy-turvy results make no sense.

Second, the majority's conception of a reasonable worker is unclear. Although the majority first states that its test is whether a "reasonable worker" might well be dissuaded, *ante*, at 13 (internal quotation marks omitted), it later suggests that at least some individual characteristics of the actual retaliation victim must be taken into account. The majority comments that "the significance of any given act of retaliation will often depend upon the particular circumstances," and provides the following illustration: "A schedule change in an employee's work schedule may make little difference to many workers, but may matter enormously to a young mother with school age children." *Ante*, at 14.

This illustration suggests that the majority's test is not whether an act of retaliation well might dissuade the average reasonable worker, putting aside all individual characteristics, but, rather, whether the act well might dissuade a reasonable worker who shares at least some individual characteristics with the actual victim. The majority's illustration introduces three individual characteristics: age, gender, and family responsibilities. How many more individual characteristics a court or jury may or must consider is unclear.

* * *

For these reasons, I would not adopt the majority's test but would hold that *§ 704(a)* reaches only those discriminatory practices covered by *§ 703(a)*.

IV

Applying this interpretation, I would affirm the decision of the Court of Appeals. The actions taken against respondent -- her assignment to new and substantially less desirable duties and her suspension without pay -- fall within the definition of an "adverse employment action."

* * *

I would hold that respondent's suspension without pay likewise satisfied the materially adverse employment action test. Accordingly, although I would hold that a plaintiff asserting a *§ 704(a)* retaliation claim must show the same type of materially adverse employment action that is required for a *§ 703(a)* discrimination claim, I would hold that petitioner met that standard in this case, and I, therefore, concur in the judgment.

Notes

1. There has been a sharp rise in retaliation claims over the last decade, and as you can see from Justice Breyer's opinion, lower courts had adopted a variety of different standards. What do you think accounts for the different standards and the increase in claims? And do you think the Supreme Court adopted the standard that best matches the statutory language? What about as a policy matter, how does the adopted standard fit?

2. Justice Alito's concurrence is likely to be heavily scrutinized as it represents his first opinion on discrimination issues as a Supreme Court Justice. How would you identify his primary concern? And why do you think no other Justice joined his opinion?

3. As Justice Alito highlights in his concurrence, there was a curious aspect to this case insofar as the plaintiff had prevailed under a stricter standard in the lower courts, thus, as Ms. White's attorney commented at oral argument, the plaintiff was put in a position of advocating for a standard she did not need.

Replace the discussion regarding the Ninth Circuit, including the panel's decision in *Jespersen,* at the end of Note 3 on page 412 with the following discussion:

In the Ninth Circuit, an employer's sex-differentiated appearance standard violates Title VII if it is more burdensome for one gender than another gender (the "unequal burdens" test) or if it requires one gender to conform to a stereotypical image that would objectively impede her or his ability to perform the job (the stereotyping test applied in *Price Waterhouse v. Hopkins*, 490 U.S. 228 (1989). See *Jespersen v. Harrah's Operating Co.*, 2006 U.S. App. LEXIS 9307 (9th Cir. April 14, 2006) (en banc).

Replace the first full paragraph on page 418 with the following new paragraph:

Impermissible motivation is the intent to subject plaintiff to an adverse employment action because of race, sex or other impermissible factor. The phrase "because of" is the causal link between an employee's unfavorable treatment and the employer's impermissible motivation. Thus, causation is sometimes viewed as a third element of disparate treatment discrimination. See Margaret E. Johnson, Comment, *A Unified Approach To Causation In Disparate Treatment Cases: Using Sexual Harassment By Supervisors As The Casual Nexus For The Discriminatory Motivating Factor In Mixed Motive Cases*, 1993 Wisc. L. Rev. 231 (1993). The standard of proof varies depending on the type of case: direct evidence (subsection b1)); pretext (subsection b2)); or mixed-motive (subsection b3)).

Insert the following sentence after the citation to *Bell v. Birmingham Linen Services* at the end of Note 1 on page 420:

The use of the word "boy" by a plant manager in reference to a black employee can be evidence of racial animus depending on the context in which the word was used, including the manager's inflection, tone of voice, local custom, and historical usage. *Ash v. Tyson Foods, Inc.*, 546 U.S. 454 (2006). See *Price Waterhouse v. Hopkins*, 490 U.S. 228 (1989) (sexual stereotyping constitutes direct evidence of gender bias).

Insert the following new note as Note 3 on page 420:

Must the impermissible motivation, established by direct evidence, be the determinative (or substantial) factor that causes the plaintiff's unfavorable treatment? Or need it only be a motivating factor? Because the Supreme Court in *Desert Palace v. Costa*, 539 U.S. 90, 94 n 1 (2003) refuses to decide whether § 703(m), which mandates the latter standard in mixed-motive cases, applies outside the mixed-motive context, it may be reasonable to assume that the determinative-factor test, which is applicable in pretext cases, see *Rachid v. Jack In The Box, Inc.*, 376 F. 3d 305, 310 (5th Cir. 2004), is the standard of causation for direct evidence cases.

Replace Note 1 on page 440 with the following new Note 1:

1. In *Price Waterhouse*, a plurality opinion, the impermissible factor was sexual stereotyping by some of the partners of the accounting firm, and the permissible factor was the female accountant's lack of interpersonal skills. As the discussion in *Desert Palace* suggests, Justice O'Connor's opinion concurring in the judgment is generally recognized as representing the holding in *Price Waterhouse*. See, e.g., *Anderson v. Consol. Rail Corp.*, 297 F.3d 242, 248 (3d Cir. 2002). For a critical analysis of *Price Waterhouse*, see Roy L. Brooks, *The Structure of Disparate Treatment Litigation After Hopkins*, 6 Labor Law. 215 (1990).

Replace Note 1 on page 451 with the following new Note 1:

1. The court held that the *post-Desert Palace* mixed-motive analysis used in Title VII cases "is equally applicable" to the ADEA, and that such extension "represents a merging of the *McDonnell Douglas* and *Price Waterhouse* approaches," creating what the court calls the "modified *McDonnell Douglas* approach" or "integrated approach." Under the integrated method, the plaintiff must first demonstrate a prima facie case of discrimination. Establishing a prima facie case necessarily entails the use of indirect evidence, for the introduction of direct evidence at this stage renders the *McDonnell Douglas* method inapplicable. In other words, there is no need to establish a prima facie case, which merely shifts the burden of production, when one has direct evidence of discrimination, the effect of which, as Justice O'Connor notes in her concurring opinion in *Desert Palace*, supra, is to "shift the burden of persuasion." If the plaintiff establishes a prima facie case, the defendant then must articulate a legitimate, nondiscriminatory reason for its adverse employment decision. If the defendant meets its burden of production, the plaintiff opposing a summary judgment motion must then offer sufficient evidence to create a genuine issue of material fact that either (1) the employer's reason is a pretext (i.e., prove that an impermissible factor was the determinative motivation behind the adverse employment decision) or (2) that the employer's reason, while true, is not the only one reason for its conduct (i.e., the adverse employment decision was also motivated by an impermissible factor). *Desert Palace* holds that at this (mixed-motive) stage of the evidentiary process the plaintiff can use either direct or indirect evidence to prove that the impermissible factor was but a "motivating factor" behind the adverse employment decision. Presumably, if the plaintiff had direct evidence of discrimination at the beginning, he or she could have avoided the *McDonnell Douglas* process, provided that the direct evidence could show that the impermissible factor was the *determinative factor* rather than a motivating factor in the employer's decision. Otherwise, the plaintiff would have to go through the entire *McDonnell Douglas* process before he or she could use direct evidence that showed that the impermissible factor was only a motivating factor. See, e.g., *Burrell v. Dr Pepper/Seven Up Bottling Group, LP*, 482 F.3d 408, 411-412 (5th Cir. 2007). Some lowers courts disagree with *Rachid*'s explicit holding that *Desert Palace* applies outside the Title VII context. Instead, these courts hold that the *Price Waterhouse* test, discussed in Justice O'Connor's concurring opinion in *Desert Palace*, applies in non-Title VII mixed-motive cases (e.g., ADEA or ADA cases). Thus, in these cases the plaintiff must use direct evidence to establish that the impermissible factor was the determinative, or substantial, factor behind the decision. The defendant can avoid liability here by using the same-

decision defense. See, e.g., *Fakete v. Aetna, Inc.*, 308 F.3d 335, 338 (3rd Cir. 2002); *Helfrich v. Lehigh Valley Hosp.*, 2005 U.S. Dist. LEXIS 14792 (cases discussed therein).

Insert the following new subsection 5c just before subsection 6 on page 510.

c. Was disparate Impact Theory a Mistake?

One of the co-authors of this casebook, Professor Michael Selmi raises this interesting question in a law review article, *Was the Disparate Impact Theory a Mistake?*, 53 UCLA L. Rev. 701 (2006). In this article, Professor Selmi argues that the disparate impact theory arouse not as a general theory of equality, but more modestly as a device to deal with specific instances of prior discrimination. After reviewing the cases, Professor Selmi concludes that the disparate impact theory has had limited success outside of written employment tests, and that disparate impact is extremely difficult to prove in court. Professor Selmi's most striking conclusion is that the disparate impact theory my have had the unintentional effect of undercutting the disparate treatment theory by limiting our understanding of what constitutes intentional discrimination. Our concept of intentional discrimination continues to turn on motivation and animus. The major social mistake of pushing so hard for disparate impact theory, Professor Selmi argues, was the belief that law could do the work that politics itself could not–to wit, bring about substantive racial equality. Professor Selmi argues for a greater commitment by society to remedying inequalities,

Insert the following sentence just before the last sentence on p. 545 that begins, "Like Title VII:"

A plaintiff who has no rights under an existing contract (a non-contracting party) and who was not prevented from entering into a contractual relationship with the defendant cannot sue under §1981. *Domino's Pizza, Inc. v. Mc Donald,* 126 S. Ct. 1246 (2006).

Insert the following sentences at the end of Note 5 on page 555:

In *EEOC v. Sidley Austin LLP*, 437 F.3d 695 (7th Cir. 2006), the court held that the EEOC could sue an employer to seek monetary relief on behalf of individuals who failed to file timely EEOC charges under the ADEA and, thus, were barred from bringing their own ADEA lawsuits. The court reasoned that the EEOC's enforcement authority was independent of statutory rights accorded to individuals.

CHAPTER 5

THE RIGHT TO VOTE

Add new Note 4 on p. 588:

4. In 2005, Georgia passed a law requiring voters to present a government-issued identification before voting. Over the objection of its career staff, the Department of Justice precleared the requirement, making Georgia the only state at the time to require photo identification as the sole method of identification as a condition of voting (Indiana and Missouri subsequently passed similar laws). The Georgia voting requirement, and subsequent modifications to the law, were challenged as a violation of the Equal Protection Clause, and the district court enjoined the law as denying voters the right to vote, and holding further that the state's interest in deterring voter fraud was not sufficiently narrowly tailored. See *Common Cause/Gerogia v. Billups*, 439 F. Supp. 2d 1294 (N.D. Ga. 2006). In the Georgia litigation, it was established that between 600,000 and 900,000 citizens of voting age did not have photo identification and that the elderly and minorities were disproportionately represented among those without suitable identification. Id. at 1306. Although the case involved preclearance issues, and raised questions of race, the court ultimately enjoined the statute as violating the fundamental right to vote under the Fourteenth Amendment. See also *ACLU v. Santillanes*, 2007 U.S. Dist. LEXIS 17087 (D.N.M. 2007) (enjoining Albuquerque municipal requirement for voter identification). Other courts, however, have upheld similar requirements. The Seventh Circuit Court of Appeals upheld Indiana's photo identification requirement, noting specifically that the plaintiffs had failed to identify any voter "who intends not to vote because of the new law . . . ." *Crawford v. Marion County Election Bd.*, 472 F.3d 949, 952 (7th Cir. 2007). In a vigorous dissent, Judge Evans stated: "Let's not beat around the bush: The Indiana voter photo ID law is a not-too-thinly veiled attempt to discourage election-day turnout by certain folks believed to skew Democratic." Id. at 955. In a slightly different context, the Ninth Circuit recently upheld Arizona's requirement that before they can register to vote, individuals must provide proof of citizenship. See *Gonzalez v. Arizona*, 485 F.3d 1041 (9th Cir. 2007).

Although the cases just discussed all involved state or local legislation, the voter identification issue has also generated controversy at the federal level. A federal commission, known as the Carter-Baker Commission which was created to address federal election reform, proposed requiring voter identification for federal elections. The report, which includes many other recommendations and was issued in 2005, can be viewed at http://www.american.edu/ia/cfer/report/full_report. pdf. Three members of the Commission dissented from the report based on concerns that voter identification would deter voting with a particular effect among low-income and minority voters. George Washington University Law School Professor

Spencer Overton was one of the dissenters and his views, along with the counterarguments, are presented in his article *Voter Identification*, 105 Mich. L. Rev. 631 (2007).

Add new Note 7 on p. 607:

7. An issue that has gained substantial attention of late involves the disenfranchisement of felons. Most states prohibit those convicted of felonies from voting during their incarceration and often while on parole, and some states permanently bar felons from voting. African Americans are disproportionately represented among felons and, as a result, these laws often have a disparate effect and it has also been alleged that some of the laws, particularly those passed during Reconstruction or shortly thereafter, were premised on on racial animus. In 1974, the Supreme Court rejected a challenge to felon disenfranchisement laws under the Fourteenth Amendment, and unless a plaintiff were able to establish that a law was passed with specific racial intent, claims under the Fourteenth Amendment appear to be foreclosed. See *Richardson v. Ramirez*, 418 U.S. 24 (1974). More recently, a number of challenges to the disenfranchisement laws have been filed under section 2 of the Voting Rights Act of 1965, relying on the totality of the circumstances test established in *Thornburg v. Gingles*. The en banc courts in the Second and Eleventh Circuits have recently rejected the challenges, under slightly different analyses. In *Hayden v. Pataki*, 449 F.3d 305 (2d Cir. 2006) (en banc), the Court held that challenges to felony disenfranchisement laws were not encompassed by the language of section 2, even if the laws had a disparate effect on African Americans. The four dissenting judges would have permitted a challenge under the Voting Rights Act. In *Johnson v. Bush*, 405 F.3d 1214 (11th Cir.), cert. denied, 126 S. Ct. 650 (2005), the court, with two judges dissenting, upheld Florida's law, which required individuals convicted of felonies to petition to have their rights restored. To hold otherwise, the court concluded, would conflict with the specific language of the Fourteenth Amendment that allows felony disenfranchisement. The court found that the directive of the Voting Rights Act was not sufficiently specific to override the Fourteenth Amendment. The Ninth Circuit has held to the contrary in a challenge to the State of Washington's disenfranchisement law. In reversing the district court's grant of summary judgment, the court held that statistical proof of disparate impact was sufficient to state a claim under the totality of the circumstances test of *Gingles*, and remanded for further proceedings since the lower court had rejected the statistical evidence. See *Farrakhan v. Washington*, 338 F.3d 1009 (9th Cir. 2003). On remand, the district court upheld the Washington law based on the totality of the circumstances test. See *Farrakhan v. Gregoire*, 2006 U.S. Dist. LEXIS 45987 (E.D. Wa. 2006). The issue of felon disenfranchisement has also produced an extensive body of scholarship. Two recent interesting analyses are Gabriel J. Chin, *Reconstruction, Felon Disenfranchisement, and the Right to Vote: Did the Fifteenth Amendment Repeal Section 2 of the Fourteenth Amendment?* 92 Geo. L.J. 259 (2004); Pamela S. Karlan, *Convictions and Doubts: Retribution, Representation and the Debate Over Felon Disenfranchisement*, 56 Stan. L. Rev. 1147 (2004).

In addition to racial justice concerns, there is also a pragmatic political issue present: because African Americans are so heavily burdened by the disenfranchisement rules, and because African Americans skew heavily Democratic in their voting, there is a sense that if the laws were repealed (or modified) close election results could be altered. This, of course, turns on whether the individuals currently disenfranchised would vote. A recent book has sought to estimate the likely political effect of felony disenfranchisement. Professors Jeff Manza and Christopher Uggen estimate that by denying the vote to felons, the average state disenfranchises approximately 2.4% of its voting-age population but as much as 8.4% of its voting age blacks, with some states disenfranchising as many as 20% of its voting age blacks. Based on a projected turnout rate of 27%, compared to about 52% of the general population in presidential elections, the authors estimate that allowing felons to vote would have made a difference in several significant Senate elections over the last decade, and likely would have tipped the balance in the 2000 presidential election in the contested state of Florida. See Jeff Manza & Christopher Uggen, *Locked Out: Felon Disenfranchisement and American Democracy* (2006). For a more skeptical analysis of the actual effect of the laws on elections see Thomas J. Miles, *Felon Disenfranchisement and Voter Turnout*, 33 Journal L. Studies 85 (2004).

Add the following material to the end of Note 6 on page 665:

To the surprise of many, the Voting Rights Act was extended for another twenty-five years with very little controversy and a year ahead of when the law was set to expire. The extension passed in the Senate by a vote of 98-0, and the only opposition within Congress arose from a small group of Southern legislators who questioned the need for continued federal oversight. See Hamil R. Harris & Michael Abramowitz, *Bush Signs Voting Rights Act Extension*, Wash. Post, 7/28/06, at A3.

CHAPTER 6

ADMINISTRATION OF JUSTICE

Add new Note 5 on p. 695:

5. In April 2007, the Department of Justice issued a special report regarding contacts between police and the public. The report, based on data for 2005, found that an individual's most common contact with the police came through a traffic stop. According to the report, white, African American and Hispanic drivers were all stopped at similar rates, but African Americans and Hispanic drivers were searched at significantly higher rates. In 2005, 3.6% of white drivers were searched, whereas the figure for African-American drivers was 9.5% and for Hispanic drivers, 8.8%. Police found evidence of criminal wrong-doing in 11.6% of the searches, although the report did not breakdown those searches by race or ethnicity. See Bureau of Justice Statistics, *Contacts Between Police and the Public, 2005* (April 2007).

Add the following material to the end of Note 2 on p. 731:

The Supreme Court decided *Miller-El v. Dretke*, 545 U.S. 231 (2005) at the end of the 2004 Term. In a 6-3 decision, with an opinion authored by Justice Souter, the Supreme Court held that the prosecutor's office ran afoul of the Equal Protection clause with its peremptory strikes. The Court began its analysis by stating: "The numbers describing the prosecution's use of peremptories are remarkable. Out of 20 black members of the 108-person venire panel for Miller-El's trial, only 1 served. Although 9 were excused for cause or by agreement, 10 were peremptorily struck by the prosecution. The prosecutors used their peremptory strikes to exclude 91% of the eligible African-American venire members . . . . Happenstance is unlikely to produce this disparity." Id. at 241 (internal citations omitted). From there, the Court engaged in a close review of the record, paying particular attention to disparate questioning afforded white jurors. The Court also expressed substantial skepticism regarding the prosecution's proferred reasons, noting: "It is true that peremptories are often the subjects of instinct, *Batson v. Kentucky,* 476 U.S., at 106 (Marshall, J., concurring), and it can sometimes be hard to say what the reason is. But when illegitimate grounds like race are in issue, a prosecutor simply has got to state his reasons as best he can and stand or fall on the plausibility of the reasons he gives. A *Batson* challenge does not call for a mere exercise in thinking up any rational basis. If the stated reason does not hold up, its pretextual significance does not fade because a trial judge, or an appeals court, can imagine a reason that might not have been shown up as false." Id. at 252. The Court also found evidence of racial discrimination in the way the prosecutors had manipulated the jury cards to push African Americans to the rear of the jury pool, different voir dire questions asked of white and black jurors, and the history of discrimination in the Dallas County prosecutor's office.

In a concurring opinion, Justice Breyer, writing only for himself and echoing earlier views of Justice Marshall, questioned the continued wisdom of permitting peremptory challenges:

> In *Batson v. Kentucky,* 476 U.S. 79 (1986), the Court adopted a burden-shifting rule designed to ferret out the unconstitutional use of race in jury selection. In his separate opinion, Justice Thurgood Marshall predicted that the Court's rule would not achieve its goal. The only way to "end the racial discrimination that peremptories inject into the jury-selection process," he concluded, was to "eliminat[e] peremptory challenges entirely." *Id.,* at 102-103 (concurring opinion). Today's case reinforces Justice Marshall's concerns. . . .
>
> To begin with, this case illustrates the practical problems of proof that Justice Marshall described. As the Court's opinion makes clear, Miller-El marshaled extensive evidence of racial bias. But despite the strength of his claim, Miller-El's challenge has resulted in 17 years of largely unsuccessful and protracted litigation – including 8 different judicial proceedings and 8 different judicial opinions, and involving 23 judges, of whom 6 found the *Batson* standard violated and 16 the contrary.
>
> The complexity of this process reflects the difficulty of finding a legal test that will objectively measure the inherently subjective reasons that underlie use of a peremptory challenge. . . . *Batson* asks judges to engage in the awkward, sometime hopeless, task of second-guessing a prosecutor's instinctive judgment – the underlying basis for which may be invisible even to the prosecutor exercising the challenge. See 476 U.S., at 106 (Marshall, J., concurring) (noting that the unconscious internalization of racial stereotypes may lead litigants more easily to conclude "that a prospective black juror is 'sullen,' or 'distant,'" even though that characterization would not have sprung to mind had the prospective juror been white); see also Page, *Batson*'s Blind-Spot: Unconscious Stereotyping and the Peremptory Challenge, *85 B. U. L. Rev. 155, 161 (2005)* ("'[s]ubtle forms of bias are automatic, unconscious, and unintentional'" and "'escape notice, even the notice of those enacting the bias'" (quoting Fiske, What's in a Category?: Responsibility, Intent, and the Avoidability of Bias Against Outgroups, in The Social Psychology of Good and Evil 127 (A. Miller ed. 2004))). In such circumstances, it may be impossible for trial courts to discern if a "'seat-of-the-pants'" peremptory challenge reflects a "'seat-of-the-pants'" racial stereotype. *Batson,* 476 U.S., at 106 (Marshall, J., concurring) (quoting *id.* 530 U.S. 133, 138 (Rehnquist, J., dissenting)).
>
> Given the inevitably clumsy fit between any objectively measurable standard and the subjective decisionmaking at issue, I am not surprised to find studies and anecdotal reports suggesting that, despite *Batson,* the discriminatory use of peremptory challenges remains

a problem. See, *e.g.*, Baldus, Woodworth, Zuckerman, Weiner, & Broffitt, The Use of Peremptory Challenges in Capital Murder Trials: A Legal and Empirical Analysis, 3 U. Pa. J. Const. L. 3, 52-53, 73, n. 197 (2001) (in 317 capital trials in Philadelphia between 1981 and 1997, prosecutors struck 51% of black jurors and 26% of nonblack jurors; defense counsel struck 26% of black jurors and 54% of nonblack jurors; and race-based uses of prosecutorial peremptories declined by only 2% after *Batson*); Rose, The Peremptory Challenge Accused of Race or Gender Discrimination? Some Data from One County, 23 Law and Human Behavior 695, 698-699 (1999) (in one North Carolina county, 71% of excused black jurors were removed by the prosecution; 81% of excused white jurors were removed by the defense); Tucker, In Moore's Trials, Excluded Jurors Fit Racial Pattern, Washington Post, Apr. 2, 2001, p A1 (in D. C. murder case spanning four trials, prosecutors excused 41 blacks or other minorities and 6 whites; defense counsel struck 29 whites and 13 black venire members) . . . .

Practical problems of proof to the side, peremptory challenges seem increasingly anomalous in our judicial system. On the one hand, the Court has widened and deepened *Batson*'s basic constitutional rule. It has applied *Batson*'s antidiscrimination test to the use of peremptories by criminal defendants, *Georgia v. McCollum,* 505 U.S. 42 (1992), by private litigants in civil cases, *Edmonson v. Leesville Concrete Co.,* 500 U.S. 614 (1991), and by prosecutors where the defendant and the excluded juror are of different races, *Powers v. Ohio,* 499 U.S. 400 (1991). It has recognized that the Constitution protects not just defendants, but the jurors themselves. *Id., at 409.* And it has held that equal protection principles prohibit excusing jurors on account of gender. See *J. E. B. v. Alabama ex rel. T. B., 511 U.S. 127 (1994).* Some lower courts have extended *Batson*'s rule to religious affiliation as well. See, *e.g., United States v. Brown,* 352 F.3d 654, 668-669 (CA2 2003); *State v. Hodge,* 726 A.2d 531, 553 (1999) . . .

On the other hand, the use of race- and gender-based stereotypes in the jury-selection process seems better organized and more systematized than ever before. See, *e.g.*, Post, A Loaded Box of Stereotypes: Despite 'Batson,' Race, Gender Play Big Roles in Jury Selection., Nat. L. J., Apr. 25, 2005, pp 1, 18 (discussing common reliance on race and gender in jury selection). For example, one jury-selection guide counsels attorneys to perform a "demographic analysis" that assigns numerical points to characteristics such as age, occupation, and marital status – in addition to race as well as gender. See V. Starr & A. McCormick, Jury Selection 193-200 (3d ed. 2001). Thus, in a hypothetical dispute between a white landlord and an African-American tenant, the authors suggest awarding two points to an African-American venire member while subtracting one point from her white counterpart. *Id.*, at 197-199. . . .

For example, materials from a legal convention, while noting that "nationality" is less important than "once was thought," and emphasizing that "the answers a prospective juror gives to questions are much more valuable," still point out that "[s]tereotypically" those of "Italian, French, and Spanish" origin "are thought to be pro-plaintiff as well as other minorities, such as Mexican and Jewish[;] [p]ersons of German, Scandinavian, Swedish, Finnish, Dutch, Nordic, British, Scottish, Oriental, and Russian origin are thought to be better for the defense"; African-Americans "have always been considered good for the plaintiff," and "[m]ore politically conservative minorities will be more likely to lean toward defendants." Blue, Mirroring, Proxemics, Nonverbal Communication and Other Psychological Tools, Advocacy Track--Psychology of Trial, Association of Trial Lawyers of America Annual Convention Reference Materials, 1 Ann. 2001 ATLA-CLE 153, available at WESTLAW, ATLA-CLE database (June 8, 2005). . . .

These examples reflect a professional effort to fulfill the lawyer's obligation to help his or her client. . . . Nevertheless, the outcome in terms of jury selection is the same as it would be were the motive less benign. And as long as that is so, the law's antidiscrimination command and a peremptory jury-selection system that permits or encourages the use of stereotypes work at cross-purposes.

Finally, a jury system without peremptories is no longer unthinkable. Members of the legal profession have begun serious consideration of that possibility. See, *e.g., Alen v. Florida,* 596 So. 2d 1083, 1088-1089 (Fla. App. 1992) (Hubbart, J., concurring); Broderick, Why the Peremptory Challenge Should Be Abolished, 65 Temp. L. Rev. 369 (1992) (authored by Senior Judge on the U. S. District Court for the Eastern District of Pennsylvania); Hoffman, Peremptory Challenges Should be Abolished: A Trial Judge's Perspective, *64 U. Chi. L. Rev. 809 (1997)* (authored by a Colorado state-court judge); Altschuler, The Supreme Court and the Jury: Voir Dire, Peremptory Challenges, and the Review of Jury Verdicts, *56 U. Chi. L. Rev. 153, 199-211 (1989)*; Amar, Reinventing Juries: Ten Suggested Reforms, *28 U. C. D. L. Rev. 1169, 1182-1183 (1995).* And England, a common-law jurisdiction that has eliminated peremptory challenges, continues to administer fair trials based largely on random jury selection. See Criminal Justice Act, 1988, ch. 33, § 118(1), 22 Halsbury's Statutes 357 (4th ed. 2003 reissue) (U. K.) . . . .

I recognize that peremptory challenges have a long historical pedigree. They may help to reassure a party of the fairness of the jury. But long ago, Blackstone recognized the peremptory challenge as an "arbitrary and capricious species of [a] challenge." 4 W. Blackstone, Commentaries on the Laws of England 346 (1769). If used to express stereotypical judgments about race, gender, religion, or national origin, peremptory challenges betray the jury's democratic origins and undermine its representative function. . . . The "scientific" use of peremptory challenges may also contribute to public cynicism about the fairness of the jury system and its role in American government. See, *e.g.,* S. O'Connor, Juries: They May Be Broke, But We Can Fix Them, Chautauqua Institution Lecture, July 6, 1995. And, of course, the right to a jury free of discriminatory taint is

> constitutionally protected--the right to use peremptory challenges is not. See *Stilson v. United States,* 250 U.S. 583, 586 (1919) . . .
>
> Justice Goldberg, dissenting in *Swain v. Alabama, 380 U.S. 202 (1965)*, wrote, "Were it necessary to make an absolute choice between the right of a defendant to have a jury chosen in conformity with the requirements of the Fourteenth Amendment and the right to challenge peremptorily, the Constitution compels a choice of the former." *Id.,* at 244; see also *Batson,* 476 U.S., at 107 (Marshall, J., concurring) (same); *Edmonson,* 500 U.S., at 630 *(KENNEDY, J.)* ("[I]f race stereotypes are the price for acceptance of a jury panel as fair, the price is too high to meet the standard of the Constitution"). This case suggests the need to confront that choice. In light of the considerations I have mentioned, I believe it necessary to reconsider *Batson*'s test and the peremptory challenge system as a whole.

Id. at 266-273 (Breyer, J., concurring).

CHAPTER 7

CONSTITUTIONAL TORTS

Add the following at the end of Note 4 on p. 804:

In another car chase in which the police chose to ram a fleeing car to knock it off the road, rather than ending the pursuit, the Court found the tactic reasonable and therefore consistent with the strictures of the Fourth Amendment. See *Scott v. Harris*, 127 S. Ct. 1769 (2007). This case was notable, in part, because the Supreme Court posted a video of the car chase on its website adding, "We are happy to allow the videotape to speak for itself." Id. at 1775 at n.5. (The video can be seen at www.supremecourtus.gov/opinions/video/scott_v_harris.rmvb.)

Add the following new case on p. 814:

Town of Castle Rock v. Gonzales

545 U.S. 748 (2005)

SCALIA, J., delivered the opinion of the Court, in which REHNQUIST, C. J., and O'CONNOR, KENNEDY, SOUTER, THOMAS, and BREYER, JJ., joined. SOUTER, J., filed a concurring opinion, in which BREYER, J., joined. STEVENS, J., filed a dissenting opinion, in which GINSBURG, J., joined.

[750] JUSTICE SCALIA delivered the opinion of the Court.

We decide in this case whether an individual who has obtained a state-law restraining order has a constitutionally [751] protected property interest in having the police enforce the restraining order when they have probable cause to believe it has been violated.

I

The horrible facts of this case are contained in the complaint that respondent Jessica Gonzales filed in Federal District Court. (Because the case comes to us on appeal from a dismissal of the complaint, we assume its allegations are true. See *Swierkiewicz v. Sorema N. A.,* 534 U.S. 506, 508, n. 1 (2002).) Respondent alleges that petitioner, the town of Castle Rock, Colorado, violated the Due

Process Clause of the Fourteenth Amendment to the United States Constitution when its police officers, acting pursuant to official policy or custom, failed to respond properly to her repeated reports that her estranged husband was violating the terms of a restraining order.

The restraining order had been issued by a state trial court several weeks earlier in conjunction with respondent's divorce proceedings. The original form order, issued on May 21, 1999, and served on respondent's husband on June 4, 1999, commanded him not to "molest or disturb the peace of [respondent] or of any child," and to remain at least 100 yards from the family home at all times. 366 F.3d 1093, 1143 (CA10 2004) (en banc) (appendix to dissenting opinion of O'Brien, J.). The bottom of the pre-printed form noted that the reverse side contained "IMPORTANT NOTICES FOR RESTRAINED PARTIES AND LAW ENFORCEMENT OFFICIALS." *Ibid.* (emphasis deleted). The preprinted [752] text on the back of the form included the following "**WARNING**":

> "**A KNOWING VIOLATION OF A RESTRAINING ORDER IS A CRIME** . . . . A VIOLATION WILL ALSO CONSTITUTE CONTEMPT OF COURT. **YOU MAY BE ARRESTED** WITHOUT NOTICE IF A LAW ENFORCEMENT OFFICER HAS PROBABLE CAUSE TO BELIEVE THAT YOU HAVE KNOWINGLY VIOLATED THIS ORDER." *Id.,* at 1144.

The preprinted text on the back of the form also included a "**NOTICE TO LAW ENFORCEMENT OFFICIALS**," which read in part:

> "YOU SHALL USE EVERY REASONABLE MEANS TO ENFORCE THIS RESTRAINING ORDER. YOU SHALL ARREST, OR, IF AN ARREST WOULD BE IMPRACTICAL UNDER THE CIRCUMSTANCES, SEEK A WARRANT FOR THE ARREST OF THE RESTRAINED PERSON WHEN YOU HAVE INFORMATION AMOUNTING TO PROBABLE CAUSE THAT THE RESTRAINED PERSON HAS VIOLATED OR ATTEMPTED TO VIOLATE ANY PROVISION OF THIS ORDER AND THE RESTRAINED PERSON HAS BEEN PROPERLY SERVED WITH A COPY OF THIS ORDER OR HAS RECEIVED ACTUAL NOTICE OF THE EXISTENCE OF THIS ORDER." *Ibid.*

* * *

[753] According to the complaint, at about 5 or 5:30 p.m. on Tuesday, June 22, 1999, respondent's husband took the three daughters while they were playing outside the family home. No advance arrangements had been made for him to see the daughters that evening. When respondent noticed the children were missing, she suspected her husband had taken them. At about 7:30 p.m., she called the Castle Rock Police Department, which dispatched two officers. The complaint continues:

"When [the officers] arrived . . ., she showed them a copy of the TRO and requested that it be enforced and the three children be returned to her immediately. [The officers] stated that there was nothing they could do about the TRO and suggested that [respondent] call the Police Department again if the three children did not return home by 10:00 p.m." App. to Pet. for Cert. 126a.

At approximately 8:30 p.m., respondent talked to her husband on his cellular telephone. He told her "he had the three children [at an] amusement park in Denver." *Ibid.* She called the police again and asked them to "have someone check for" her husband or his vehicle at the amusement park and "put out an [all points bulletin]" for her husband, but the officer with whom she spoke "refused to do so," again telling her to "wait until 10:00 p.m." and see if "her husband returned the girls." *Id.,* at 126a-127a.

At approximately 10:10 p.m., respondent called the police and said her children were still missing, but she was now told to wait until midnight. She called at midnight and told the dispatcher her children were still missing. She went to her husband's apartment and, finding nobody there, called the police at 12:10 a.m.; she was told to wait for an officer to arrive. When none came, she went to the police station at [754] 12:50 a.m. and submitted an incident report. The officer who took the report "made no reasonable effort to enforce the TRO or locate the three children. Instead, he went to dinner." *Id.,* at 127a.

At approximately 3:20 a.m., respondent's husband arrived at the police station and opened fire with a semiautomatic handgun he had purchased earlier that evening. Police shot back, killing him. Inside the cab of his pickup truck, they found the bodies of all three daughters, whom he had already murdered. *Ibid.*

On the basis of the foregoing factual allegations, respondent brought an action under Rev. Stat. § 1979, 42 U.S.C. §1983, claiming that the town violated the Due Process Clause because its police department had "an official policy or custom of failing to respond properly to complaints of restraining order violations" and "tolerated the non-enforcement of restraining orders by its police officers." App. to Pet. for Cert. 129a. The complaint also alleged that the town's actions "were taken either willfully, recklessly or with such gross negligence as to indicate wanton disregard and deliberate indifference to" respondent's civil rights. *Ibid.*

Before answering the complaint, the defendants filed a motion to dismiss under Federal Rule of Civil Procedure 12(b)(6). The District Court granted the motion, concluding that, whether construed as making a substantive due process or procedural due process claim, respondent's complaint failed to state a claim upon which relief could be granted.

A panel of the Court of Appeals affirmed the rejection of a substantive due process claim, but found that respondent had alleged a cognizable procedural due process claim. 307 F.3d 1258 (CA10 2002). On rehearing en banc, a divided [755] court reached the same disposition, concluding that respondent had a "protected property interest in the enforcement of the terms of her restraining order" and that the town had deprived her of due process because "the police never 'heard' nor seriously entertained her request to enforce and protect her interests in the restraining order." 366 F.3d at 1101, 1117. We granted certiorari. 543 U.S. 955, 125 S. Ct. 417 (2004).

II

The Fourteenth Amendment to the United States Constitution provides that a State shall not "deprive any person of life, liberty, or property, without due process of law." Amdt.14, § 1. In 42 U.S.C. §1983, Congress has created a federal cause of action for "the deprivation of any rights, privileges, or immunities secured by the Constitution and laws." Respondent claims the benefit of this provision on the ground that she had a property interest in police enforcement of the restraining order against her husband; and that the town deprived her of this property without due process by having a policy that tolerated nonenforcement of restraining orders.

As the Court of Appeals recognized, we left a similar question unanswered in *DeShaney v. Winnebago County Dep't of Social Servs.,* 489 U.S. 189 (1989), another case with "undeniably tragic" facts: Local child-protection officials had failed to protect a young boy from beatings by his father that left him severely brain damaged. *Id.,* at 191-193. We held that the so-called "substantive" component of the Due Process Clause does not "require the State to protect the life, liberty, and property of its citizens against invasion by private actors." *Id.,* at 195. We noted, however, that the petitioner had not properly preserved the argument that – and we thus "declined to consider" whether -- state "child protection statutes gave [him] an 'entitlement' to receive protective services in accordance with the terms of the statute, an entitlement which would enjoy due process protection." *Id.,* at 195, n. 2.

[756] The procedural component of the Due Process Clause does not protect everything that might be described as a "benefit": "To have a property interest in a benefit, a person clearly must have more than an abstract need or desire" and "more than a unilateral expectation of it. He must, instead, have a legitimate claim of entitlement to it." *Board of Regents of State Colleges v. Roth,* 408 U.S. 564, 577 (1972). Such entitlements are "'of course, . . . not created by the Constitution. Rather, they are created and their dimensions are defined by existing rules or understandings that stem from an independent source such as state law.'" *Paul v. Davis,* 424 U.S. 693, 709 (1976) . . . .

A

Our cases recognize that a benefit is not a protected entitlement if government officials may grant or deny it in their discretion. See, *e.g., Kentucky Dep't of Corrections v. Thompson,* 490 U.S. 454, 462-463 (1989). The Court of Appeals in this case determined that Colorado law created an entitlement to enforcement of the restraining order because the "court-issued restraining order . . . specifically dictated that its terms must be enforced" and a "state statute commanded" enforcement of the order when certain objective conditions were met (probable cause to believe that the order had been violated and that the object of the order had received notice of its existence). 366 F.3d at 1101, n. 5. Respondent contends that we are obliged "to give deference to the Tenth Circuit's analysis of Colorado law on" whether she had an entitlement to enforcement of the restraining order. Tr. of Oral Arg. 52.

We will not, of course, defer to the Tenth Circuit on the ultimate issue: whether what Colorado law has given respondent constitutes a property interest for purposes of the Fourteenth Amendment. That determination, despite its state-law [757] underpinnings, is ultimately one of federal constitutional law. "Although the underlying substantive interest is created by 'an independent source such as state law,' federal constitutional law determines whether that interest rises to the level of a 'legitimate claim of entitlement' protected by the Due Process Clause." *Memphis Light, Gas & Water Div. v. Craft,* 436 U.S. 1, 9 (1978) (emphasis added) (quoting *Roth, supra,* at 577). Resolution of the federal issue begins, however, with a determination of what it is that state law provides. In the context of the present case, the central state-law question is whether Colorado law gave respondent a right to police enforcement of the restraining order. It is on this point that respondent's call for deference to the Tenth Circuit is relevant.

We have said that a "presumption of deference [is] given the views of a federal court as to the law of a State within its jurisdiction." *Phillips, supra,* at 167. That presumption can be overcome, however, see *Leavitt v. Jane L.,* 518 U.S. 137, 145 (1996) *(per curiam),* and we think deference inappropriate here. The Tenth Circuit's opinion, which reversed the Colorado District Judge, did not draw upon a deep well of state-specific expertise, but consisted primarily of quoting language from the restraining order, the statutory text, and a state-legislative-hearing transcript. See 366 F.3d at 1103-1109. These texts, moreover, say nothing distinctive to Colorado, but use mandatory language that (as we shall discuss) appears in many state and federal statutes. As for case law: the only state-law cases about restraining orders that the Court of Appeals relied upon were decisions of Federal District Courts in Ohio and Pennsylvania and state courts in New Jersey, Oregon, and Tennessee. *Id.,* at 1104-1105, n. 9, 1109. Moreover, if we were simply to accept [758] the Court of Appeals' conclusion, we would necessarily have to decide conclusively a federal constitutional question (*i.e.*, whether such an entitlement constituted property under the Due Process Clause *and*, if so, whether petitioner's customs or policies provided too little process to protect it). We proceed, then, to our own analysis of whether Colorado law gave respondent a right to enforcement of the restraining order.

B

The critical language in the restraining order came not from any part of the order itself (which was signed by the state-court trial judge and directed to the restrained party, respondent's husband), but from the preprinted notice to law-enforcement personnel that appeared on the back of the order. See *supra,* at 2-3. That notice effectively restated the statutory provision describing "peace officers' duties" related to the crime of violation of a restraining order. At the time of the conduct at issue in this case, that provision read as follows:

"(a) Whenever a restraining order is issued, the protected person shall be provided with a copy of such [759] order. *A peace officer shall use every reasonable means to enforce a restraining order.*

"*(b) A peace officer shall arrest, or, if an arrest would be impractical under the circumstances, seek a warrant for the arrest of a restrained person* when the peace officer has information amounting to probable cause that:

"(I) The restrained person has violated or attempted to violate any provision of a restraining order; and

"(II) The restrained person has been properly served with a copy of the restraining order or the restrained person has received actual notice of the existence and substance of such order.

"(c) In making the probable cause determination described in paragraph (b) of this subsection (3), a peace officer shall assume that the information received from the registry is accurate. *A peace officer shall enforce a valid restraining order whether or not there is a record of the restraining order in the registry.*" Colo. Rev. Stat. § 18-6-803.5(3) (Lexis 1999) (emphases added).

The Court of Appeals concluded that this statutory provision -- especially taken in conjunction with a statement from its legislative history, and with another statute restricting [760] criminal and civil liability for officers making arrests -- established the Colorado Legislature's clear intent "to alter the fact that the police were not enforcing domestic abuse retraining orders," and thus its intent "that the recipient of a domestic abuse restraining order have an entitlement to its enforcement." 366 F.3d at 1108. Any other result, it said, "would render domestic abuse restraining orders utterly valueless." *Id.,* at 1109.

This last statement is sheer hyperbole. Whether or not respondent had a right to enforce the restraining order, it rendered certain otherwise lawful conduct by her husband both criminal and in contempt of court. See § § 18-6-803.5(2)(a), (7). The creation of grounds on which he could be arrested, criminally prosecuted, and held in contempt was hardly "valueless" -- even if the prospect of those sanctions ultimately failed to prevent him from committing three murders and a suicide.

We do not believe that these provisions of Colorado law truly made enforcement of restraining orders *mandatory.* A well established tradition of police discretion has long coexisted with apparently mandatory arrest statutes. [761]

* * *

The deep-rooted nature of law-enforcement discretion, even in the presence of seemingly mandatory legislative commands, is illustrated by *Chicago v. Morales,* 527 U.S. 41 (1999), which involved an ordinance that said a police officer "'shall order'" persons to disperse in certain circumstances, *id.,* at 47, n. 2. This Court rejected out of hand the possibility that "the mandatory language of the ordinance . . . afforded the police *no* discretion." *Id.,* at 62, n. 32. It is, the Court proclaimed, simply "common sense that *all* police officers must use some discretion in deciding when and where to enforce city ordinances." *Ibid.* (emphasis added).

Against that backdrop, a true mandate of police action would require some stronger indication from the Colorado Legislature than "shall use every reasonable means to enforce a restraining order" (or even "shall arrest . . . or . . . seek a warrant"), § § 18-6-803.5(3)(a), (b). . . . It is hard to imagine that a Colorado peace officer would not have some discretion to determine that – despite probable cause to believe a restraining order has been violated -- the circumstances of the violation or the competing duties of that officer or his agency counsel decisively against enforcement in a particular instance. [762] The practical necessity for discretion is particularly apparent in a case such as this one, where the suspected violator is not actually present and his whereabouts are unknown. Cf. *Donaldson v. Seattle,* 831 P.2d 1098, 1104 (1992) ("There is a vast difference between a mandatory duty to arrest [a violator who is on the scene] and a mandatory duty to conduct a follow up investigation [to locate an absent violator] . . . . A mandatory duty to investigate would be completely open-ended as to priority, duration and intensity.").

* * *

[763] Respondent does not specify the precise means of enforcement that the Colorado restraining-order statute assertedly mandated -- whether her interest lay in having police arrest her husband, having them seek a warrant for his arrest, or having them "use every reasonable means, up to and including arrest, to enforce the order's terms," Brief for Respondent 29-30. Such indeterminacy is not the hallmark of a duty that is mandatory. Nor can someone be safely deemed "entitled" to something when the identity of the alleged entitlement is vague [764]. . . . The dissent . . . ultimately contends that the obligations under the statute were quite precise: either make an arrest or (if that is impractical) seek an arrest warrant. The problem with this is that the seeking of an arrest warrant would be an entitlement to nothing but procedure -- which we have held inadequate even to support standing, see *Lujan v. Defenders of Wildlife,* 504 U.S. 555 (1992); much less can it be the basis for a property interest. After the warrant is sought, it remains within the discretion of a judge whether to grant it, and after it is granted, it remains within the discretion of the police whether and when to execute it. Respondent would have been assured nothing but the seeking of a warrant. This is not the sort of "entitlement" out of which a property interest is created.

Even if the statute could be said to have made enforcement of restraining orders "mandatory" because of the domestic-violence context of the underlying statute, that would not [765] necessarily mean that state law gave *respondent* an entitlement to *enforcement* of the mandate. Making the actions of government employees obligatory can serve various legitimate ends other than the conferral of a benefit on a specific class of people. See, *e.g., Sandin v. Conner,* 515 U.S. 472, 482 (1995) (finding no constitutionally protected liberty interest in prison regulations phrased in mandatory terms, in part because "such guidelines are not set forth solely to benefit the prisoner"). The serving of public rather than private ends is the normal course of the criminal law because criminal acts, "besides the injury [they do] to individuals, . . . strike at the very being of society; which cannot possibly subsist, where actions of this sort are suffered to escape with impunity." 4 W. Blackstone, Commentaries on the Laws of England 5 (1769) . . . .

Respondent's alleged interest stems only from a State's *statutory* scheme -- from a restraining order that was authorized by and tracked precisely the statute on which the Court of Appeals relied. She does not assert that she has any common-law or contractual entitlement to enforcement. If she was given a statutory entitlement, we would expect to see some indication of that in the statute itself. . . . [766] The creation of a personal entitlement to something as vague and novel as enforcement of restraining orders cannot "simply go without saying." *Post,* at 788, n. 16 (STEVENS, J., dissenting). We conclude that Colorado has not created such an entitlement.

C

Even if we were to think otherwise concerning the creation of an entitlement by Colorado, it is by no means clear that an individual entitlement to enforcement of a restraining order could constitute a "property" interest for purposes of the Due Process Clause. Such a right would not, of course, resemble any traditional conception of property. Although that alone does not disqualify it from due process protection, as *Roth* and its progeny show, the right to have a restraining order enforced does not "have some ascertainable monetary value," as even our *"Roth*-type property-as-entitlement" cases have implicitly required. Merrill, The Landscape of Constitutional Property, *86 Va. L. Rev. 885, 964 (2000).* Perhaps most radically, the alleged property [767] interest here arises *incidentally,* not out of some new species of government benefit or service, but out of a function that government actors have always performed -- to wit, arresting people who they have probable cause to believe have committed a criminal offense.

The indirect nature of a benefit was fatal to the due process claim of the nursing-home residents in *O'Bannon v. Town Court Nursing Center,* 447 U.S. 773 (1980). We held that, while the withdrawal of "direct benefits" (financial payments under Medicaid for certain medical services) triggered due process protections, *id.,* at 786-787, the same was not true for the "indirect benefits" conferred on Medicaid patients when the Government enforced "minimum standards of care" for nursing-home facilities, *id.,* at 787. "An indirect and incidental result of the Government's enforcement action . . . does not amount to a deprivation of any interest in life, liberty, or property." *Ibid.* . . . [768]

III

We conclude, therefore, that respondent did not, for purposes of the Due Process Clause, have a property interest in police enforcement of the restraining order against her husband. It is accordingly unnecessary to address the Court of Appeals' determination that the town's custom or policy prevented the police from giving her due process when they deprived her of that alleged interest.

In light of today's decision and that in *DeShaney,* the benefit that a third party may receive from having someone else arrested for a crime generally does not trigger protections under the Due Process Clause, neither in its procedural nor in its "substantive" manifestations. This result reflects our continuing reluctance to treat the Fourteenth Amendment as "'a font of tort law,'" *Parratt v. Taylor,*

451 U.S. 527, 544 (1981) (quoting *Paul v. Davis,* 424 U.S., at 701), but it does not mean States are powerless to provide victims with personally enforceable remedies. Although the framers of the Fourteenth Amendment and the Civil Rights Act of 1871, 17 Stat. 13 (the original source of § 1983), did not create a system by which police departments are generally held financially accountable for crimes that better policing might have [769] prevented, the people of Colorado are free to craft such a system under state law. Cf. *DeShaney,* 489 U.S., at 203.

The judgment of the Court of Appeals is Reversed.

JUSTICE SOUTER, with whom JUSTICE BREYER joins, concurring.

I agree with the Court that Jessica Gonzales has shown no violation of an interest protected by the Fourteenth Amendment's Due Process Clause, and I join the Court's opinion. . . . [771] The Due Process Clause extends procedural protection to guard against unfair deprivation by state officials of substantive state-law property rights or entitlements; the federal process protects the property created by state law. But Gonzales claims a property interest in a state-mandated process in and of itself. This argument is at odds with the rule that "process is not an end in itself. Its constitutional purpose is to protect a substantive interest to which the individual has a legitimate claim of entitlement." *Olim v. Wakinekona,* 461 U.S. 238, 250 (1983). . . . In putting to rest the notion that the scope of an otherwise discernible property interest could be limited by related state-law procedures, this Court observed that "the categories of substance and procedure are distinct . . . . 'Property' cannot be defined by the procedures provided for its deprivation." *Cleveland Bd. of Ed. v. Loudermill,* 470 U.S. 532, 541 (1985). . . . [772] There is no articulable distinction between the object of Gonzales's asserted entitlement and the process she desires in order to protect her entitlement; both amount to certain steps to be taken by the police to protect her family and herself. Gonzales's claim would thus take us beyond *Roth* or any other recognized theory of Fourteenth Amendment due process, by collapsing the distinction between property protected and the process that protects it, and would federalize every mandatory state-law direction to executive officers whose performance on the job can be vitally significant to individuals affected. . . .

[773] JUSTICE STEVENS, with whom JUSTICE GINSBURG joins, dissenting.

The issue presented to us is much narrower than is suggested by the far-ranging arguments of the parties and their *amici*. Neither the tragic facts of the case, nor the importance of according proper deference to law enforcement professionals, should divert our attention from that issue. That issue is whether the restraining order entered by the Colorado trial court on June 4, 1999, created a "property" interest that is protected from arbitrary deprivation by the Due Process Clause of the Fourteenth Amendment.

It is perfectly clear, on the one hand, that neither the Federal Constitution itself, nor any federal statute, granted respondent or her children any individual entitlement to police protection. See *DeShaney v. Winnebago County Dep't of Social Servs.,* 489 U.S. 189 (1989). On the other hand, it is equally clear that federal law imposes no impediment to the creation of such an entitlement by

Colorado law. Respondent certainly could have entered into a contract with a private security firm, obligating the firm to provide protection to respondent's family; respondent's interest in such a contract would unquestionably constitute "property" within the meaning of the Due Process Clause. If a Colorado statute enacted for her benefit, or a valid order entered by a Colorado judge, created the functional equivalent of such a private contract by granting respondent an entitlement to mandatory individual protection by the local police force, that state-created right would also qualify as "property" entitled to constitutional protection. . . .[774]

The central question in this case is therefore whether, as a matter of Colorado law, respondent had a right to police assistance comparable to the right she would have possessed to any other service the government or a private firm might have undertaken to provide. . . .

There was a time when our tradition of judicial restraint would have led this Court to defer to the judgment of more qualified tribunals in seeking the correct answer to that difficult question of Colorado law. Unfortunately, although the majority properly identifies the "central state-law question" in this case as "whether Colorado law gave respondent a right to police enforcement of the restraining order, " *ante,* at 8, it has chosen to ignore our settled practice by providing its *own* answer to that question. . . .[775]

I

The majority's decision to plunge ahead with its own analysis of Colorado law imprudently departs from this Court's longstanding policy of paying "deference [to] the views of a federal court as to the law of a State within its jurisdiction." *Phillips v. Washington Legal Foundation,* 524 U.S. 156, 167 (1998). This policy is not only efficient, but it reflects "our belief that district courts and courts of appeal are better schooled in and more able to interpret the laws of their respective States." *Brockett v. Spokane Arcades, Inc.,* 472 U.S. 491, 500-501 (1985). Accordingly, we have declined to show deference only in rare cases in which the court of appeal's resolution of state law was "clearly wrong" or otherwise seriously deficient. See *Brockett,* 472 U.S., at 500, n. 9.

Unfortunately, the Court does not even attempt to demonstrate that the six-judge en banc majority was "clearly wrong" in its interpretation of Colorado's domestic restraining order statute; nor could such a showing be made. For it is certainly *plausible* to construe "*shall* use every reasonable means to enforce a restraining order" and "*shall* arrest," Colo. Rev. Stat. §§ 18-6-803.5(3)(a)-(b) (Lexis 1999) (emphases added), as conveying mandatory directives to the police, particularly when the same statute, at other times, tellingly employs different language that suggests police discretion, see § 18-6-803.5(6)(a) ("A peace officer *is authorized to* use every reasonable means to protect . . . "; "Such peace officer *may* transport . . . " (emphases added)). Moreover, unlike today's decision, the Court of Appeals was attentive to the legislative history of the statute, focusing on a statement by the statute's sponsor in the Colorado House, *ante,* at 10, n. 6 (quoting statement), which it took to "emphasize the importance of the police's mandatory enforcement of domestic restraining orders." 366 F.3d 1093, 1107 (CA10 2004) (en banc). Far from overlooking the traditional presumption of police discretion, then, the Court of Appeals' diligent analysis of the statute's text, purpose, and history led it to conclude that the Colorado Legislature intended precisely to abrogate that presumption in the specific context of domestic restraining orders. That conclusion is eminently reasonable and, I believe, worthy of our deference.[2]

II

* * * [776]

III

[779] Three flaws in the Court's rather superficial analysis ofthe merits highlight the unwisdom of its decision to answer the state-law question *de novo*. First, the Court places undue weight on the various statutes throughout the country that seemingly mandate police enforcement but are generally understood to preserve police discretion. As a result, the Court gives short shrift to the unique case of "mandatory arrest" statutes in the domestic violence context; States passed a wave of these statutes in the 1980's and 1990's with the unmistakable goal of eliminating police discretion in this area. Second, the Court's formalistic analysis fails to take seriously the fact that the Colorado statute at issue in this case was enacted for the benefit of the narrow class of persons who are beneficiaries of domestic restraining orders, and that the order at issue in this case was specifically intended to provide protection to respondent and her children. Finally, the Court is simply wrong to assert that a citizen's interest in the government's commitment to provide police enforcement in certain defined circumstances does not resemble any "traditional conception of property," *ante*, at 17; in fact, a citizen's property interest in such a commitment is just as concrete and worthy of protection as her interest in any other important service the government or a private firm has undertaken to provide.

In 1994, [780] the Colorado General Assembly passed omnibus legislation targeting domestic violence. . . . In adopting this legislation, the Colorado General Assembly joined a nationwide movement of States that took aim at the crisis of police underenforcement in the domestic violence sphere by implementing "mandatory arrest" statutes. The crisis of underenforcement had various causes, not least of which was the perception by police departments and police officers that domestic violence was a private, "family" matter and that arrest was to be used as a last resort. Sack, Battered Women and the State: The Struggle for the Future of Domestic Violence Policy, *2004 Wis. L. Rev. 1657, 1662-1663* (hereinafter Sack); *id., at 1663* ("Because these cases were considered noncriminal, police assigned domestic violence calls low priority and often did not respond to them for several

---

[2] The Court declines to show deference for the odd reason that, in its view, the Court of Appeals did not "draw upon a deep well of state-specific expertise," *ante*, at 8, but rather examined the statute's text and legislative history and distinguished arguably relevant Colorado case law. See *ante*, at 8-9, and n. 4. This rationale makes a mockery of our traditional practice, for it is precisely when there is no state law on point that the presumption that circuits have local expertise plays any useful role. When a circuit's resolution of a novel question of state law is grounded on a concededly complete review of all the pertinent state-law materials, that decision is entitled to deference. . . .

hours or ignored them altogether"). In response to these realities, and emboldened by a well-known 1984 experiment by the Minneapolis police department, "many states enacted mandatory [781] arrest statutes under which a police officer must arrest an abuser when the officer has probable cause to believe that a domestic assault has occurred or that a protection order has been violated." Developments in the Law: Legal Responses to Domestic Violence, *106 Harv. L. Rev. 1528, 1537 (1993)*. The purpose of these statutes was precisely to "counter police resistance to arrests in domestic violence cases by removing or restricting police officer discretion; mandatory arrest policies would increase police response and reduce batterer recidivism." *Sack 1670.*

Thus, when Colorado passed its statute in 1994, it joined the ranks of 15 States that mandated arrest for domestic violence offenses and 19 States that mandated arrest for domestic restraining order violations. See Developments in the Law, *106 Harv. L. Rev., at 1537, n. 68* (noting statutes in 1993) . . . .

Given the specific purpose of these statutes, there can be no doubt that the Colorado Legislature used the term [782] "shall" advisedly in its domestic restraining order statute. While "shall" is probably best read to mean "may" in other Colorado statutes that seemingly mandate enforcement, cf. Colo. Rev. Stat. § 31-4-112 (Lexis 2004) (police "*shall suppress* all riots, disturbances or breaches of the peace, *shall apprehend* all disorderly persons in the city . . . " (emphases added)), it is clear that the elimination of police discretion was integral to Colorado and its fellow States' solution to the problem of underenforcement in domestic violence cases. . . .

While Colorado case law does not speak to the question, it is instructive that other state courts interpreting their analogous statutes have not only held that they eliminate the police's traditional discretion to refuse enforcement, but have [783] also recognized that they create rights enforceable against the police under state law. For example, in *Nearing v. Weaver,* 670 P.2d 137 (1983) (en banc), the court held that although the common law of negligence did not support a suit against the police for failing to enforce a domestic restraining order, the statute's mandatory directive formed the basis for the suit because it was "a specific duty imposed by statute for the benefit of individuals previously identified by judicial order." *Id., at 140.* In *Matthews v. Pickett County,* 996 S.W.2d 162 (Tenn. 1999) (on certification to the Sixth Circuit), the court confirmed that the statute mandated arrest for violations of domestic restraining orders, and it held that the "public duty" defense to a negligence action was unavailable to the defendant police officers because the restraining order had created a "special duty" to protect the plaintiff. *Id.,* at 165. See also *Campbell v. Campbell,* 294 N. J. Super. 18, 24, 682 A.2d 272, 274 (1996) (domestic restraining order statute "allows no discretion" with regard to arrest; "the duty imposed on the police officer is ministerial"); *Donaldson v. Seattle,* 65 Wn. App. 661, 670, 831 P.2d 1098, 1103 (1992) ("Generally, where an officer has legal grounds to make an arrest he has considerable discretion to do so. In regard to domestic violence, the rule is the reverse. If the officer has the legal grounds to arrest pursuant to the statute, he has a mandatory duty to make the arrest"). To what extent the Colorado Supreme Court [784] would agree with the views of these courts is, of course, an open question, but it does seem rather brazen for the majority to assume that the Colorado Supreme Court would repudiate this consistent line of persuasive authority from other States.

Indeed, the Court fails to come to terms with the wave of domestic violence statutes that provides the crucial context for understanding Colorado's law. The Court concedes that, "in the specific context of domestic violence, mandatory-arrest statutes have been found in some States to be more mandatory than traditional mandatory-arrest statutes," *ante*, at 13, but that is a serious understatement. The difference is not a matter of degree, but of kind. Before this wave of statutes, the legal rule was one of discretion; as the Court shows, the "traditional," general mandatory arrest statutes have always been understood to be "mandatory" in name only, see *ante*, at 11. The innovation of the domestic violence statutes was to make police enforcement, not "more mandatory," but simply *mandatory*. If, as the Court says, the existence of a protected "entitlement" turns on whether "government officials may grant or deny it in their discretion," *ante*, at 7, the new mandatory statutes undeniably create an entitlement to police enforcement of restraining orders.

Perhaps recognizing this point, the Court glosses over the dispositive question -- whether the police enjoyed discretion to deny enforcement -- and focuses on a different question -- which "precise means of enforcement," *ante*, at 14, were called for in this case. But that question is a red herring. The statute directs that, upon probable cause of a violation, "a peace officer shall arrest, or, if an arrest would be impractical under the circumstances, seek a warrant for the arrest of a restrained person." Colo. Rev. Stat. § 18-6-803.5(3)(b) (Lexis 1999). Regardless of whether the enforcement called for in this case was arrest or the seeking of an arrest warrant (the answer to that question probably changed over the course of the night as the respondent gave the police more information about the husband's whereabouts), the crucial point is that, under the statute, the police were *required* to provide enforcement; *they lacked the discretion to do nothing. . . .* [785]

* * *

[788] Because the statute's guarantee of police enforcement is triggered by, and operates only in reference to, a judge's granting of a restraining order in favor of an identified "protected person," there is simply no room to suggest that such a person has received merely an "'incidental'" or "indirect" benefit, see *ante*, at 18. As one state court put it, domestic restraining order statutes "identify with precision when, to whom, and under what circumstances police protection must be afforded. The legislative purpose in requiring the police to enforce individual restraining orders clearly is to protect the named persons for whose protection the order is issued, not to protect the community at large by general law enforcement activity." *Nearing,* 670 P. 2d, at 143. . . .[789]

IV

Given that Colorado law has quite clearly eliminated the police's discretion to deny enforcement, respondent is correct that she had much more than a "unilateral expectation" that the restraining order would be enforced; rather, she had a "legitimate claim of entitlement" to enforcement. *Roth, 408 U.S., at 577.* Recognizing respondent's property interest in the enforcement of her restraining order is fully consistent with our precedent. . . . [O]ur cases have found "property" interests in a number of state-conferred benefits and services, including welfare benefits, *Goldberg v. Kelly,* 397 U.S. 254 (1970);

disability benefits, *Mathews v. Eldridge,* 424 U.S. 319 (1976); public education, *Goss v. Lopez,* 419 U.S. 565 (1975); utility services, *Memphis Light, Gas & Water Div. v. Craft,* 436 U.S. 1 (1978); government employment, *Cleveland Bd. of Ed. v. [790]Loudermill,* 470 U.S. 532 (1985); as well as in other entitlements that defy easy categorization, see, *e.g.*, *Bell v. Burson,* 402 U.S. 535 (1971) (due process requires fair procedures before a driver's license may be revoked pending the adjudication of an accident claim); *Logan,* 455 U.S., at 431 (due process prohibits the arbitrary denial of a person's interest in adjudicating a claim before a state commission).

Police enforcement of a restraining order is a government service that is no less concrete and no less valuable than other government services, such as education. The relative novelty of recognizing this type of property interest is explained by the relative novelty of the domestic violence statutes creating a mandatory arrest duty; before this innovation, the unfettered discretion that characterized police enforcement defeated any citizen's "legitimate claim of entitlement" to this service. Novel or not, respondent's claim finds strong support in the principles that underlie our due process jurisprudence. In this case, Colorado law *guaranteed* the provision of a certain service, in certain defined circumstances, to a certain class of beneficiaries, and respondent reasonably relied on that guarantee. . . . [791] Surely, if respondent had contracted with a private security firm to provide her and her daughters with protection from her husband, it would be apparent that she possessed a property interest in such a contract. Here, Colorado undertook a comparable obligation, and respondent -- with restraining order in hand -- justifiably relied on that undertaking. Respondent's claim of entitlement to this promised service is no less legitimate than the other claims our cases have upheld, and no less concrete than a hypothetical agreement with a private firm. The fact that it is based on a statutory enactment and a judicial order entered for her special protection, rather than on a formal contract, does not provide a principled basis for refusing to consider it "property" worthy of constitutional protection.[20]

[792] V

Because respondent had a property interest in the enforcement of the restraining order, state officials could not deprive her of that interest without observing fair procedures. Her description of the police behavior in this case and the department's callous policy of failing to respond properly to reports of restraining order violations clearly alleges [793] a due process violation. At the very least, due process requires that the relevant state decisionmaker *listen* to the claimant and then *apply the relevant criteria* in reaching his decision. The failure to observe these minimal procedural safeguards

---

[20] According to JUSTICE SOUTER, respondent has asserted a property interest in merely a "state-mandated process," *ante*, at 3 (opinion concurring in part and concurring in judgment), rather than in a state-mandated "substantive guarantee," *ibid*. . . . Enforcement of a restraining order is a tangible, substantive act. If an estranged husband violates a restraining order by abducting children, and the police succeed in enforcing the order, the person holding the restraining order has undeniably just received a substantive benefit. As in other procedural due process cases, respondent is arguing that the police officers failed to follow fair procedures in ascertaining whether the statutory criteria that trigger their obligation to provide enforcement -- *i.e.*, an outstanding order plus probable cause that it is being violated -- were satisfied in her case. . . .

creates an unacceptable risk of arbitrary and "erroneous deprivations," *Mathews,* 424 U.S., at 335 . . . .

Accordingly, I respectfully dissent.

Notes

1. This was a difficult, and close, case. What factors do you think were most significant in determining the outcome of the case? Who has the better reading of the statute?

2. As you work your way through the chapter, you will see some common themes develop in the cases, themes of federalism, and a concern with turning common torts into constitutional issues. How do those themes play out in the *Gonzales* case?

3. As the dissent discusses, many jurisdictions moved to policies that required mandatory arrests in the context of domestic abuse, or for enforcing protection orders. These policies were intended to counter traditional police reluctance to get involved in what was frequently defined as a "domestic problem," and have often proved controversial. These, and other related policies have been the subject of a tremendous amount of scrutiny and scholarship. For two recent comprehensive discussions of the policies, and the surrounding literature, see Deborah Epstein, *Procedural Justice: Tempering the State's Response to Domestic Violence*, 43 Wm. & Mary L. Rev. 1843 (2002) and G. Kristin Miccio, *A House Divided: Mandatory Arrest, Domestic Violence, and the Conservatization of the Battered Women's Movement*, 42 Hous. L. Rev. 237 (2005).

Add new Note 5 on p. 915

The Supreme Court recently held that a plaintiff who obtains a preliminary injunction but ultimately loses the case on the merits is not a prevailing party for purposes of obtaining attorney's fees. See *Sole v. Wyner*, 127 S. Ct. 2188 (2007). In *Sole*, the plaintiff challenged the state's rule that required patrons of state parks to wear bathing suits so that she could present what she described as an antiwar artwork consisting of nude individuals assembled into a peace sign. The plaintiff obtained a preliminary injunction the day after the complaint was filed, and displayed the peace sign at a park on Valentine's day with a screen to shield those who did not want to witness the nudity. Thereafter, the plaintiff lost her request for a permanent injunction, in part because many of those participating in the Valentine's day display failed to remain behind the screen. Even though the plaintiff had obtained preliminary relief sufficient to allow her to display her work, in a unanimous opinion written by Justice Ginsburg the Court found that she was not entitled to any attorney's fees. "Prevailing party status," the Court explained, "does not attend achievement of a preliminary injunction that is reversed, dissolved, or otherwise undone by the final decision in the same case." Id. at 2195 (footnote omitted). The Court, however, reserved judgment on whether obtaining a preliminary injunction, without a contrary final ruling, "may sometimes warrant an award of counsel fees." Id. at 2196.

CHAPTER 8

THE RIGHTS OF LANGUAGE MINORITIES

Add the following after the last full paragraph on page 928:

Xenophobic preoccupation with "national identity" has persisted, and immigrants continue to be painted as the culprits threatening "the American way of life," failing to assimilate into some nationalistic notion of "American culture." Samuel Huntington, *Who Are We? The Challenges to National Identity* 171-77 (2004). What such perspectives fail to consider, however, is that "[t]he available empirical evidence shows that, in the aggregate, immigrants from all nations, including Mexico, . . . learn English, exhibit high labor participation rates, are firmly committed to family, and participate in community life in ways comparable to other Americans. This is not surprising given that most immigrants come to the United States because they embrace American political values and economic freedoms." Kevin R. Johnson & Bill Ong Hing, *National Identity in a Multicultural Nation: The Challenge of Immigration Law and Immigrants* (book review), 103 Mich. L. Rev. 1347, 1351-52 (2005) (footnotes omitted).

Add the following before *Bernal v. Fainter* on page 978:

In *LeClerc v. Webb*, 419 F.3d 405 (5th Cir. 2005), *cert. denied*, 2007 WL 1802961 (2007), nonimmigrant aliens were prevented by a Louisiana Supreme Court Rule from sitting for the Louisiana Bar, despite being otherwise qualified. After *Graham v. Richardson*, 403 U.S. 365 (1971) [excerpted in text at p. 1022], the Court has used "strict scrutiny to invalidate state laws affecting 'resident aliens' or 'permanent resident aliens,'" when evaluating claims of Equal Protection violations. Id. at 416. However, the court suggested that, in reviewing all other alienage classifications, only rational basis has been used. Id. (but see *Plyler v. Doe*, 457 U.S. 202 (1982) [excerpted in text at p. 1076]. The *LeClerc* court noted that resident aliens are entitled to preferential standing, in contrast to nonimmigrant aliens, because permanent resident aliens are similar to citizens, with the exception that they are unable to participate in the political process. Id. at 417.

Conversely, nonimmigrant aliens have no legitimate claim to permanent residence and generally have no intention of abandoning their native citizenship. Id. Because of their temporary and varied status, nonimmigrant aliens are not a discrete or insular class in the same way that resident aliens are. Id. at 418. The court stated that "the Supreme Court has yet expressly to bestow equal protection status on nonimmigrant aliens." Id. at 419. The Court found *Plyler* not to be applicable to this case because being denied a work license while temporarily in the country is not analogous to children being denied basic education. Id. at 421. Therefore, rational basis was the proper standard of review. Because the rule banning nonimmigrant aliens from sitting for the bar was rationally related to the legitimate state interest of regulating those admitted to the Bar, the court found the rule to be valid. Id. at 421, 422. The court said that the law was aimed at assuring "clients that attorneys licensed by the Louisiana Bar will provide continuity and accountability in legal representation." Id. at 421. The court stated that, because of the terminable status of nonimmigrant aliens, the Bar would have difficulty in monitoring and disciplining nonimmigrant attorneys. Id.

Add the following before the last paragraph on page 1000:

Maldonado v. City of Altus, 433 F.3d 1294 (10th Cir. 2006), is another case involving a public defendant. Hispanic employees brought suit against the city of Altus, Oklahoma (the city) after it implemented an English-only policy, which prevented the speaking of other languages by city employees while at work. The plaintiffs alleged that the policy had a disparate impact under Title VII, and that the policy abridged the plaintiffs' equal protection and free speech rights, violations cognizable under the Civil Rights Act of 1871 (42 U.S.C. § 1983). Each claim was dismissed by the district court, and the plaintiffs appealed.

The protections of Title VII extend to preventing any discriminatory acts that create a hostile workplace. Id. at 1304. The Court noted that "the very fact that the city would forbid Hispanics from using their preferred language could reasonably be construed as an expression of hostility to Hispanics." Id. at 1305. Additionally, the English-only policy subjected plaintiffs to ethnic taunting and made them feel like second-class citizens, both of which tended to create a hostile work environment. Id.

The EEOC has promulgated 29 C.F.R. § 1606.7, which provides that "[a]n English-only rule that applies at all times is considered a burdensome term and condition of employment" while "an English-only rule that applies only at certain times does not violate Title VII if the employer can justify the rule by showing [a] business necessity." Id. The court observed that, if the justification for the policy is not readily apparent, it is reasonable to infer that the policy was enacted out of animosity. Id. When the defendant was unable to produce evidence that the use of other languages created communication, safety, or morale problems, the court determined that the defendant did not have a business justification for the policy and reversed the summary judgment. Id. at 1306.

The court of appeals decided that the Title VII claim could proceed but found that the plaintiffs were unable to establish a free speech violation because they did not show that the precluded speech involved matters of public concern. Id. at 1310. First, the plaintiffs failed to show that the denial of the use of Spanish was tantamount to a denial of expression. Id. at 1311. Second, the plaintiffs did not establish that, by speaking Spanish, they had intended to convey matters of public concern or "to communicate ethnic pride or opposition to discrimination." Id. The court noted that there was no constitutional protection for internal feelings, such as pride, which are not expressed, but only for communications. Id.. Therefore, even if the plaintiffs felt ethnic pride when speaking in their native tongue, the conversations would not be protected unless the listener understood that the speech was spoken to convey such pride. Id.

Furthermore, the court found *Yniguez v. Arizonans for Official English* to be inapplicable because the provision at issue in *Yniguez* applied to all members of the public, regardless of their ability to understand English. In contrast, the policy in *Altus* only applied to plaintiff city employees, all of whom were bilingual. Id. at 1312. While affirming the summary judgment in favor of the defendants on the First Amendment claim, the court iterated that, if plaintiffs had produced evidence establishing that their use of Spanish had been to communicate matters of public concern, the court may have ruled differently. Id. Cf. *Burlington N. & Santa Fe Railway Co. V. White*, 126 S. Ct. 2405 (2006) in Chapter 4 of this Supplement.

Add as new Note 3 on page 1013:

In investigating a national origin discrimination charge against Technocrest, the Equal Employment Opportunity Commission (EEOC) issued an administrative subpoena for documents relating not just to the filing parties but also for documents relating to every Filipino employee. After Technocrest refused to comply, the District Court ordered a partial enforcement of the subpoena. On appeal, Technocrest relied on *Espinoza v. Farah Manufacturing Company*, 414 U.S. 86, 89 (1973) [excerpted in text at p. 969], claiming that immigration status and citizenship [were] irrelevant to national origin discrimination. However, in affirming the district court's ruling, the court of appeals noted that the Court in *Espinoza* recognized that citizenship may be relevant to the larger picture of national origin discrimination, and that the requested documents would be relevant to determining whether Technocrest had discriminated on the basis of national origin against the class of Filipino employees as a whole. *Equal Employment Opportunity Commission v. Technocrest Systems, Inc.*, 448 F.3d 1035 (8th Cir. 2006).

Add the following as new subsection c. The Racketeer Influenced Corrupt Organizations Act (RICO), at page 1013:

In *Williams v. Mohawk Indust., Inc,* 314 F.Supp.2d 1333 (N.D. Ga. 2004), current and former employees of Mohawk Industries brought suit, claiming Mohawk violated state and federal RICO laws by employing undocumented aliens. The plaintiffs alleged that Mohawk had conspired with recruiting agencies to drive down the cost of labor by hiring and harboring undocumented workers. Id. at 1255. The plaintiffs claimed that Mohawk hired undocumented aliens from the border, assisted in their efforts to avoid detection, and then destroyed related documents. Id.

On interlocutory appeal, the court of appeals held that the plaintiffs established all of the elements of a RICO claim. The court held that, despite being distinct entities, Mohawk and the recruiters appeared to be engaged "in a conspiracy to bring illegal workers into this country for Mohawk's benefit. As such the complaint sufficiently alleges an enterprise under RICO." *Williams v. Mohawk Industries*, 411 F.3d

1252, 1258 (11th Cir. 2005). This holding is in direct conflict with a Seventh Circuit decision based on similar facts. *Baker v. IBP, Inc.*, 373 F.3d 685 (7th Cir. 2004). In *Baker*, employees brought a class action alleging that Baker had conspired with recruiters to drive down employee wages by hiring undocumented aliens in violation of RICO. Id. at 691. Unlike the decision in *Mohawk*, the *Baker* Court found that the plaintiffs were unable to establish a RICO violation because the employer and the recruiters were not engaged in a common endeavor. Id. The court found the goals of the parties to be divergent because the employer was seeking to lower wages, while the recruiters were attempting to make more money. Id. Conversely, in *Mohawk*, the Eleventh Circuit held that "there has never been any requirement that the common purpose of the enterprise be the sole purpose of each and every member of the enterprise." *Mohawk, 411 F.3d at 1259*. The court found that, despite having different goals, Mohawk and the recruiters had the common purpose of providing Mohawk with undocumented workers, thus establishing a RICO violation. Id.

Mohawk appealed the holding of the court of appeals, and the Supreme Court granted a writ of *certiorari* limited to the issue of "[w]hether a defendant corporation and its agents can constitute an 'enterprise' under the Racketeer Influenced and Corrupt Organizations Act, 18 U.S.C. §§ 1961-1968 ("RICO"), in light of the settled rule that a RICO defendant must 'conduct' or 'participate in' the affairs of some larger enterprise and not just its own affairs." *Mohawk Industries v. Williams, 126 S.Ct. 830 (2005), quoting* Pet. for a Writ of Cert. at I. However, the writ was later vacated as improvidently granted, and the case was remanded for further consideration in light of *Anza v. Ideal Steel Supply Corp*, 126 S.Ct. 1991 (2006).

On remand, the court of appeals held that the complaint sufficiently alleged a pattern of racketeering activity, conduct of an enterprise, injury to plaintiffs' business interest, and proximate cause. The court held further that the plaintiffs had standing under RICO and that the employerwas not unjustly enriched. *Williams v. Mohawk Industries*, 465 F.3d 1277 (11th Cir. 2006), *cert. denied*, 127 S. Ct. 1381 (2007).

Add the following at the end of page 1090:

On appeal, the preliminary injunction was dissolved and the judgment vacated. The court of appeals held that plaintiff state and local employees lacked standing because they failed to establish any imminent threat of prosecution for failing to report undocumented aliens who tried to obtain public benefits. *Friendly House v. Napolitano*, 419 F.3d 930 (9th Cir. 2005).

CHAPTER 9

THE RIGHTS OF PEOPLE WITH DISABILITIES

Replace the paragraph in the middle of page 1093 with the following two new paragraphs:

Others are not so sanguine. The National Institute on Disability and Rehabilitation Research reports that 79% of disabled persons who want to work are not working; middle-income families who are unable to provide expensive, ongoing treatment for their severely disabled children must somehow get poor (e.g., by breaking up families) to qualify for Medicaid; and the list goes on. See, e.g., David Armstrong, *Fear of Flying: Disabled Travelers Say Discrimination Is Still a Problem at Airlines*, Wall Street Journal, 5/9/01 at A1; *Albert R. Hunt, An Army of Opposition to Disability Rights*, Wall Street Journal, 3/15/01, at A19. Others report that the employment rate among all disabled persons has declined since the ADA. See, e.g., Julie L. Kotchkiss, "A Closer Look at the Employment Impact of the Americans with Disabilities Act," Georgia State University (Paper Presentation, February 2002). There are at least three reasons, commentators argue, that help to explain why the ADA's promise of equal employment opportunity has largely gone unfulfilled. "First, the purposefully broad language adopted by Congress has been interpreted so narrowly by courts that it rarely protects the people for whose benefit it was adopted. [the author cites in particular *Sutton v. United Air Lines, Inc.*, 527 U. S. 471 (1999) and *Albertsons, Inc., v. Kirkingburg*, 537 U. S. 555 (1999), both presented in Section C4, infra]. Second, there is evidence that courts are abusing summary judgment standards in ADA cases, which has resulted in a staggering bias in favor of employer-defendants. Finally, despite the history of disability law in the United States, there is a persistent refusal of courts to recognize that the basis of disability rights is civil rights, which results in misinterpretation of the ADA and inconsistent judgments in factually similar situations." Melanie Winegar, Note: *Big Talk, Broken Promises: How Title I of the Americans with Disabilities Act Failed Disabled Workers*, 34 Hofstra L. Rev. 1267, 1267-1268 (2006). Some have suggested that Congress "revisit the promises it made in the ADA" and "rewrite the statute to protect people who can work but whose disabilities have been excluded from the statute by the courts." As to "people whose disabilities make it difficult to work, even with an accommodation, anti-discrimination law cannot have much of an effect on employment rates except as part of a comprehensive policy encompassing social security, health care, training programs and tax incentives." Scott C. Burris and Kathryn Moss, *The Employment Discrimination Provisions of the Americans with Disabilities Act: Implementation and Impact*, available at http://ssrn.com/abstract=977256 (2007).

The ADA's implementation problems are not limited to Title I (employment). Despite federal laws protecting the voting rights of disabled Americans, the latter are still denied "access to polling places" and the right to "secret and independent voting." Michael Waterstone, *Constitutional and Statutory Voting Rights for People with Disabilities*,14 Stan. L. & Pol. Rev. 353, 354 (2003). And how is it possible to ignore the compelling story of a paraplegic who had to leave his wheelchair and crawl two flights of stairs to attend a mandatory court hearing. See *Tennessee v. Lane*, 541 U. S. 509 (2004).

Add the following citation after the first sentence in Note 6 on page 1102:

See Harry Bruinius, *Better for All the World: The Secret History of Forced Sterilization and America's Quest for Racial Purity* (2006) (giving a figure of 65,000).

Add the following new Note 7 on page 1131:

7. If parents or a school district believe that an IEP is not appropriate, the IDEA gives them the right to seek an administrative "impartial due process hearing." § 1415(f). At the hearing, all parties may be accompanied by counsel, present evidence, cross-examine, and compel the attendance of witnesses, but the statute is silent as to which party should bear the burden of proof at an administrative hearing. In *Schaffer ex rel. Schaffer v. Weast*, 546 U.S. 49 (2005), the Court held that the burden of persuasion in an administrative hearing challenging an IEP is placed upon the party seeking relief. The Court did not comment on permanent placement of the burden on the school district, which several states had already done by statute or regulation. The Third Circuit has interpreted *Schaffer* as generally applicable to all aspects of a challenged IEP. *L.E. v. Ramsey Bd. of Educ.*, 435 F.3d 384 (2006). Parents enjoy rights under the IDEA and, as a result, they can prosecute IDEA claims on their own behalf in court with or without legal representation. *Winkelman v. Parma City Sch. Dist.*, 127 S. Ct. 1994 (2007). However, § 1415(i)(3)(B) of the statute, which permits a court to "award reasonable attorneys' fees as part of costs" to prevailing parents, does not include expert fees, e.g., educational consultants used during the proceedings. The unambiguous statutory language simply adds attorneys' fees to recoverable costs set forth in the general costs statute, 28 U.S.C. § 1920, and does not give states clear notice that their acceptance of federal IDEA funds obligates them to compensate prevailing parents for expert fees. Without the recovery of expert fees, the educational experts needed to help parents obtain additional services from school districts make it very difficult, if not impossible, for low-income parents to mount a successful fight for their disabled children.

Add the following new Note 10 on page 1151:

10. Can actions against a parent exercising IDEA rights on behalf of child support a retaliation claim under Section 504? In *Bradley ex rel. Bradley v. Arkansas Dept. Of Educ.*, 443 F.3d 965 (8th Cir. 2006), the court suggested that adverse action against a parent trying to guarantee a child's right to a free appropriate education might support a Section 504 claim if there is a causal connection between the parent's lawful efforts and the adverse action. The court, however, found no causal connection between the father's requests for IDEA due process hearings and criminal charges filed by school employees stemming from the father's physical threats and other unlawful behavior. Regardless of whether claims asserting rights of disabled children are brought pursuant to IDEA, ADA, or Section 504 of Rehabilitation

Act, they must first be exhausted in state administrative proceedings. *M.T.V. v. Dekalb County School Dist.*, 446 F.3d 1153 (11th Cir. 2006).

For causation in a retaliation claim, see also, *Mershon v. St. Louis University*, 442 F.3d 1069 (8th Cir.2006) (banning disabled student from campus because of reasonable belief that student might harm faculty member did not support retaliation claim).

CHAPTER 10

AFFIRMATIVE ACTION

Add the following sentences at the end of Note 9 on page 1299:

For an intense debate over empirical data concerning the value and effectiveness of affirmative action in law schools, see, e.g., Richard H. Sander, *A Systemic Analysis of Affirmative Action in American Law Schools*, 57 Stan. L. Rev. 367 (2004); David L. Chambers et al., *The Real Impact of Ending Affirmative Action in American Law Schools: An Empirical Critique of Richard Sander's Study,* 57 Stan. L. Rev. 1855 (2005); Ian Ayres & Richard Brooks, *Does Affirmative Action Reduce the Number of Black Lawyers?,* 57 Stan. L. Rev. 1807 (2005); Richard Sander, *A Reply to Critiques*, 57 Stan. L. Rev. 1963 (2005); Richard O. Lempert, *Affirmative Action in American Law Schools: A Critical Response to Richar Sander's "A Reply to Critics,"* University of Michigan, John M. Olin Center for Law & Economics Working Paper 60 (February 24, 2006).

Add the following sentence at the end of Note 2 on page 1311:

In *Roberto v. Dept of Navy*, 440 F.3d 1341 (Fed. Cir. 2006), the court ruled that under the Veterans' Preference Act (VPA), a 'preference eligible' federal employee who has lost his job is generally entitled to certain reemployment priority rights. See U.S.C. §3315(a).